TAKING YOUR

CW00631851

STUDENT HANDBOOKS

TAKING YOUR A-LEVELS

How to achieve the results you really need

Bradley Lightbody

How To Books

Cartoons by Mike Flanagan

British Library Cataloguing in Publication Data
A catalogue record for this book is available from the British Library.

© Copyright 1996 by Bradley Lightbody.

First published in 1996 by How To Books Ltd, Plymbridge House, Estover
Road, Plymouth PL6 7PZ, United Kingdom. Tel: (01752) 202301.
Fax: (01752) 202331.

Note: The material contained in this book is set out in good faith for
general guidance and no liability can be accepted for loss or expense
incurred as a result of relying in particular circumstances on statements
made in the book. The laws and regulations are complex and liable to change,
and readers should check the current position with the relevant authorities
before making personal arrangements.

Produced for How To Books by Deer Park Productions.
Typeset by PDQ Typesetting, Stoke-on-Trent, Staffs.
Printed and bound by The Cromwell Press, Broughton Gifford, Melksham,
Wiltshire.

Contents

List of Illustrations

Preface

Welcome to your *Taking Your A-Levels* study guide. This guide provides a clear action programme on how to study for a GCE A-Level course.

Studying A-Levels involves:

- taking notes in lessons

- taking notes from textbooks

- reading and extracting key information

- conducting experiments

- writing concise essays and reports

- researching and presenting coursework

- debating key topics in class

- presenting data in graphs and tables

- drawing diagrams

- learning and remembering

- using correct English

- preparing for examinations.

Your ability in all of these skill areas will be crucial to whether you pass A-Level and to the achievement of your final grade. Developing and refining these study skills should be your immediate goal. They go across all A-Level subjects and form an important part of A-Level study. Long after you have forgotten many of the key topics from your subjects you will still retain and be able to deploy these skills at university and in later employment. In many respects these skills are the hallmark of successful A-Level students and graduates, so take action to consciously develop these skills.

The first three chapters of this guide are of immediate interest and relevance to anyone just starting A-Level but read the remaining chapters as and when you need to. In other words this is not a textbook to be read at one sitting and put on the shelf to gather dust! Instead this is an active guide to how to succeed at A-Level which should be followed as you encounter different course demands. The chapter on essay writing should be studied carefully as you approach your first essays and revisited before writing every essay until your marks and reports indicate a high level of achievement. Likewise turn to the coursework chapter before attempting any coursework and so on.

Make this guide work for you by using it regularly throughout your two year A-Level course and put into action the study techniques described and you will not be disappointed.

Finally, aim to become a Study Manager and take charge of your studies and get it right first time, every time!

Bradley Lightbody

1
Considering Your Options

In Great Britain approximately 728,000 young people reach the age of 16 each year and gain, among other rights, the right to leave school.

Approximately 556,000 of them choose to continue in full-time and part-time education and join a wide variety of academic and vocational courses. The most popular course choice is **A-Level** which is selected nationally by approximately 173,000 students.

The success rate at A-Level varies from year to year but a survey conducted by the Audit Commission in 1993 revealed the following A-Level outcomes:

- Pass grades A – E 70 per cent
- Fail grades N – U 17 per cent
- Drop out early   13 per cent.

This means that approximately 50,000 students each year fail either to complete or to pass A-Level! Apart from unforeseen circumstances why do students fail? Often it reflects:

- choosing the wrong course
- selecting the wrong subjects

but above all it reflects a lack of study skills and knowledge of how to study and how to pass.

This book is designed to ensure that you succeed not only in passing A-Level but also in gaining a Grade A award. Deciding where and what to study are perhaps your first and most difficult choices.

SELECTING WHERE TO STUDY

You can decide where to study your A-Levels and this makes you the customer. You are worth approximately £2,000 funding to whichever school or college you join, so expect to be bombarded with glossy brochures and reams of impressive statistics. Take your time to consider where to study. The choices are:

- school sixth form
- sixth form college
- further education college
- tertiary college
- private independent schools.

The proportion of 17-year-old students attending these different institutions was recorded in 1991/2 as follows:

- School sixth form   33.5 per cent
- FE College   32.6 per cent
- Independent   12.3 per cent
- Sixth form college   10.9 per cent
- Tertiary college   8.1 per cent
- Other   2.6 per cent.

(Source: Audit Commission, *Unfinished Business*, HMSO 1993, page 12.)

The above figures indicate that the majority of 17-year-old students choose to leave school and continue their education in the further education sector, but schools remain the largest single choice of institution.

The significant differences between the various institutions are as follows:

School sixth form
Sixty per cent of all schools, whether designated secondary, comprehensive or grant maintained, have a sixth form. The majority of the students will be from the relevant school but anyone may apply to join – including adults.

Sixth form college
There are 115 sixth form colleges in Great Britain and most were opened to service the 40 per cent of schools without sixth forms. In April 1993 sixth form colleges were granted 'corporation' status and now have freedom to run vocational courses and recruit adults, but the majority still specialise in A-Level courses and 16–19-year-old students.

Further education
There are 390 colleges of further education in Great Britain and they offer a wide range of vocational and academic courses for anyone over 16.

Tertiary college
A tertiary college is the designated sole provider of education courses in a given area to students aged 16 and over, and most were formed from the amalgamation of a sixth form and an FE college. They provide a full range of vocational and academic courses.

Private independent
All areas have independent, private schools which provide A-Level courses. The typical fees for one academic year are £4,000 to £5,000.

Making your choice
Your first action must be to discover the **choice of institutions** in your local area as the full choice will not exist in every local area.

All local education authorities (LEAs) provide Year 11 pupils with a post-16 options booklet and this should list all the local providers of A-Level courses. Your careers teacher at school will also be able to provide full information and, by law, must represent each choice of institution fairly. You are also entitled to a **careers interview** with a careers officer; this normally happens automatically in Year 11, but if not do ask. If you find it difficult to obtain information then telephone the Careers Service and arrange your own interview. Also ask for a copy of the *Students Charter for Further Education* as this provides detailed information on the choices open to you and some useful addresses for further information.

Once you have discovered the choice of institutions in your area you must take care to select the best place to study.

You may take some comfort from a survey of A-Level examination results in 1991 which concluded: 'The analysis found that no single type of institution appeared markedly more effective at A-Level than the others.' (Audit Commission, *Two Bs or Not. Schools/Colleges A-Level Performance 1991.*)

In addition in 1991 HM Senior Chief Inspector of Schools reported that in schools and sixth forms 82 per cent of lessons were judged to be satisfactory or better and 90 per cent in further education.

Consequently try to ignore the stereotype opinions which often brand different institutions because every college or school is different. Also ignore the opinions of family, friends and neighbours as often they are thinking back to events ten years ago or more.

Instead please attend all of the Open Evenings and:

- check the facilities on offer

- compare the examination results

- ask the **right questions.**

ASKING THE RIGHT QUESTIONS

The purpose of asking questions is to compare the choices open to you. Resist the temptation to behave like an inspector and grill the staff or headteacher on some aspect of the course provision. It is better to accept all of the literature given to you and walk around and sense the atmosphere of the school or college.

Touring the college

As you tour the school or college ask yourself:

- Is there a visible graffiti problem?

- How approachable and friendly are the staff?

- Is there evidence from noticeboards of lots regularly going on?

- Are there relevant subject displays in the classrooms?

- Are the existing students happy and content?

- Are the subject resources good?

- Is the library well resourced?

Asking questions

Study the following questions and ask those that are particularly important to you. Do not attempt to make one person answer all of these questions but instead as you tour the school or college ask questions of the different subject staff, senior staff or students as you encounter them. You might also find time to sit down and enjoy a cup of coffee and perhaps find many of the answers in the promotional leaflets and brochures.

General

1. Has there been a recent inspection?

2. Is the Inspection Report available for study?
3. What were your examination results for the past three years?
4. How is A-Level managed within the college/school?
5. How many students enrol for A-Level each year?
6. How many students on average drop out of the course early?
7. How many students on average go on to university?
8. Have you had any successful applications to Oxford or Cambridge?

Rules and regulations
1. Is there a compulsory school uniform?
2. Can you leave the school/college between lessons?
3. Is there a standard start and finish time each day?
4. Is there a compulsory assembly?
5. Is there a published discipline code and procedures?
6. Is there a Student Charter which sets out rights and responsibilities?

Subjects
1. What is the standard entry requirement for a full-time A-Level course?
2. How many subjects are offered?
3. Do you offer . . .? (Insert your subject interests.)
4. Do these subjects include coursework?
5. Do these subjects match your career plans?
6. Are there subject leaflets giving a basic syllabus outline?

Subject staff
1. Are all of the subject staff graduates in their subjects?
2. Are all of the subject staff experienced?
3. Are all of the staff teacher-trained?

Subject resources
1. Do the students have to buy subject textbooks?
2. Do the students have to buy anything else for their lessons?
3. Does each subject enjoy a comfortable classroom with adequate resources?
4. Are there sufficient supporting textbooks in the library?
5. Does the library also stock relevant videos? CD Roms? Reference Books? Magazines?

Course programme
1. Is there a compulsory wider programme of study?
2. What are the full course requirements?
3. Is A-Level General Studies compulsory?
4. Is there study skills support?
5. Is there regular tutorial support?
6. Are there workshops or extra support for Maths and English problems?
7. Is there provision to learn wordprocessing?
8. How many hours' tuition are given to each A-Level subject?
9. What is the latest class finishing time?
10. How often and what form do subject assessments take?
11. How are assessment results recorded and what follow-up takes place?
12. What careers provision exists?
13. Are there links with business or industry?
14. Are there organised visits to higher education fairs or universities?

Social considerations
1. Is there a students' union or similar organisation?
2. Is there a students' common room?
3. Are there regular social events?
4. Are there regular educational visits?
5. Is there a choice of social clubs and societies?
6. Is there a sports programme?

Once you have received answers to most of the above questions you will discover that there is no 'best' A-Level course but rather it is a case of what is **best for you**.

Select where to study on the basis of the most satisfactory answers you received to your own important considerations.

CHOOSING YOUR SUBJECTS

There are 50 different A-Level subjects to choose from and around 70 if you count the syllabus variations for subjects like History, Maths and Sciences. No school or college has the resources to offer all 70 syllabuses but you should expect a choice from around 15 different subjects with 25 + being a very high choice. All of the subjects are listed in Appendix A.

Considering AS Levels
AS Levels are half an A-Level in terms of syllabus length and examination requirements and are designed to be taken after two years' study rather than one. This creates difficulties for schools and colleges as First Year candidates may need extra teaching time to reach A-Level standard and over two years small, uneconomic classes may result. Consequently you will find a limited choice of AS subjects available in any school or sixth form and none in the smaller institutions. The value of AS is that they allow you to take a greater spread of subjects by taking two AS Levels in place of one A-Level. Some universities will require a full A-level to be studied in key subjects for the extra depth, so select with care and only after careers guidance.

Catering for all interests
Eight separate A-Level examination boards provide and examine the subject syllabuses. You may obtain full syllabus information by writing to the publications department of the relevant board or looking in your library for syllabus reference books. The names and addresses of the boards are listed in the Useful Addresses section.

The following figures taken from the Northern Examinations and Assessment Board (NEAB) Annual Report 1995 illustrate the top five and bottom five subject entries:

Top		Bottom	
General Studies	45,450	Hebrew	6
English Literature	11,242	Engineering Graphics	14
Chemistry	10,952	Ancient History	27
Biology	9,973	History of Music	45
English Language	9,224	Greek	56

Selecting subjects
Most students select three A-Level subjects as this gives entry to the full range of university degree courses. Two A-Level subjects are the **minimum entry requirement** for a university degree course but you may find that your choice of places and courses is restricted. There is no need to take four or more mainstream subject choices unless there is a particular need or interest. A fourth subject will generate a lot of extra work and may affect your overall performance. Three high grades are preferable to four mediocre grades.

Many schools and colleges make A-Level General Studies a compulsory third or fourth choice because it gives a broad general

knowledge, but remember not to count it as part of the minimum
entry requirements for university. This explains the high entry level
shown for General Studies above.

Holding the record
The *Guinness Book of Records* current record for passing the most
A-Levels with Grade A at one sitting is held by Matthew James of
Mortimer Wilson School, Derby, who gained seven Grade A passes
in 1993.

Thinking about careers
The most significant factor in selecting subjects apart from personal
interest is to ensure that your subject choices match up with your
career intentions.

Some career intentions automatically specify subjects, *eg*:

- *Doctor* – the university preference is for Maths, Biology and
  Chemistry.

Other career intentions may allow a much wider choice of subjects, *eg*:

- *Journalist* – English Language, English Literature, Communica-
  tion Studies, History, Government and Politics, Law, Classics,
  Philosophy, French, German, Sociology, Psychology, Computing,
  Economics.

It is important to discover what A-Level subjects, if any, are
specified for your career plan and also to check for any essential
GCSE requirements before finalising your subject selection. Arrange
an interview with a careers officer or consult the careers reference
books held by most school or college libraries. A careers reference
book will list all career openings along with the normal entry
requirements and preferred subjects. You should also check for any
particular university entry requirements relevant to your expected
degree course. You will find a list of useful career reference books in
the Further Reading section.

Making your final choice
If your career plans allow for a choice of subjects then make sure that
you select subjects where you have a real interest. Make the following
final checks:

- syllabus topics are of real interest

- examination pass rate is good
- tutor is enthusiastic
- good subject resources.

Finally, if after a few weeks you know you have made a mistake say so and change!

UNDERSTANDING BROCHURES AND STATISTICS

A minor revolution has taken place within education over the past ten years leading to a profusion of competing brochures and statistics:

- publication of HMI Reports
- publication of examination results
- collation of examination league tables
- publication of truancy rates
- publication of student destinations
- Parents' Charter
- Students' Charter
- removal of school catchment areas
- grant maintained schools
- independent corporation status for all colleges.

All of this information can be very confusing but you should welcome the fact that it gives you hard evidence on the achievement level of different schools. The hard part is working out what it all means!

Firstly, do not be seduced by glossy, desk top published brochures. Most schools and colleges are short of money and simply cannot afford to print commercial quality brochures. You may also find many rotting window frames and crumbling plaster-work in school buildings but this does not mean that the teaching is poor.

Main points to check

Inspections
Since the reform of HMI by the Education Act 1992 all schools are formally inspected every four years by OFSTED (the Office for

Standards in Education). The inspection reports are public and by law a copy must be produced for scrutiny upon request. The same applies to FE colleges and sixth form colleges except they are inspected by the Further Education Funding Council (FEFC). You may be presented with a summary of the inspection report but as you might expect only the good parts may be highlighted. A weak subject or a poor department may be hidden by the overall inspection results and grades. Ask if grades were awarded to the subjects you intend to take at A-Level or if you can see the actual comments made by the inspectors on these subject areas.

League tables

The national examination league tables are published every mid-November in the quality press and *The Times Educational Supplement* (TES). The league tables provide a straight listing of average A-Level points for every school and college in Great Britain. The points used are derived from the university points scoring system as explained in Appendix A.

The league tables have been condemned for not taking account of different entry qualifications and social backgrounds which will distort results. Consequently try to compare grammar with grammar and comprehensive with comprehensive *etc*.

Note the position of the schools in the rank order and against the national average.

Finally, there is no need to wait until November to see the league tables. A library will have back copies of the TES so ask for the relevant copy.

Truancy rates

Colleges do not have to produce these statistics so they will only be available for school sixth forms. Look at the total number of the students on the roll and the number reported for at least one absence. How high a percentage of the students are truants? A figure over 10 per cent should be of concern as this means that the average pupil misses a full day of school each fortnight.

Truancy rates are also reported in the national league tables so you can compare with other schools.

Destinations

The purpose of an A-Level course is mainly university entrance although many students are content to seek employment. Do most students gain a university place?

Exam results
Study any tables of exam results carefully and be concerned if the results show:

- most pass rates below 70 per cent
- high numbers of grade U results.

This implies poor recruitment and assessment monitoring.

Overall use this hard data to judge against your impressions of a school or college and to help select the best place for you. Remember that once you are satisfied that a school or college is doing its job well it is your turn. Teaching is a partnership.

CHECKING THE COURSE PROGRAMME

A-Level has been criticised many times over the past 30 years for promoting a narrow curriculum but to date it has avoided reform. To counter this criticism most schools and colleges present A-Level within a course programme. A typical course programme is as follows:

- three A-Levels
- weekly personal tutorial
- weekly study skills support
- sports and social programme
- A-Level General Studies or wider study options
- work experience placements.

You will need to check if your school or college offers A-Level within a course programme and if so which aspects are compulsory. OFSTED recommends a minimum of 12 subject choices and 80 students to maintain a satisfactory course programme.

Building up your Record of Achievement

In the competitive world of university entrance and employment this wider course programme is of value as it all feeds into producing a good Record of Achievement (ROA) and a good Personal Statement for university applicants. A ROA normally involves collating information under the following headings:

- academic progress
- skills/wider knowledge

- work experience

- social/sports interests.

The student who avoids all of these experiences will be at a disadvantage later and although grades are the most important factor everyone needs time to relax and to extend and broaden their knowledge and understanding. IT skills are particularly valued by universities as students are encouraged to wordprocess their assignments.

CHECKLIST

Consider carefully all of your options by:

- identifying all of the local institutions

- going to all of the Open Evenings

- asking the right questions

- looking at inspection reports

- examining all of the published data

- choosing subjects that really interest you

- matching subjects to your career intentions

- looking at the past examination results

- considering the resources available.

CASE STUDIES

Any adult will tell you that if they could do it all over again they would do it differently! Few people perform as well as they had hoped at school or college and apart from one celebrated case no one gets to repeat their time at A-Levels.

You can gain an advantage by following the case studies of four students all, like you, taking their A-Levels.

- Susan King, who wants to be a doctor

- Mohammed Patel, who is determined to be a journalist

- Yasmin Rawat, who wants to be a social worker

- John Stead, who is interested in business.

Learn from their mistakes and from their successes as they work through their A-Level course. Here they consider their options.

Susan meets Bob

Susan sat in the biology lab of the sixth form college and knew that it was for her. The examination results were all good and the destinations showed two recent students going on to medicine and taught by the existing science staff. She liked the set 9am to 4pm day and the range of after school activities. 'Dr Susan King, here I come,' muttered Susan to herself as she crossed the lab and patted 'Bob', the skeleton. Susan decided to study Maths, Biology and Chemistry.

Mohammed opts for school

'So I would be at no disadvantage?' questioned Mohammed. 'None', confirmed the head of the school sixth form. 'Journalists can have a wide variety of qualifications and, although we don't offer A-Level Communication Studies, our course in English Language will put you at no disadvantage.'

After more discussion and noting that his friends were also entering the school sixth form Mohammed decided to stay on too. He was comfortable at school and knew all of the staff well. The results were not as high as the local sixth form college but then it had a higher entry standard of five GSCE Grade Bs minimum compared with four Grade Cs. With hard work he would get the right results. Mohammed decided to study English Language, English Literature and History.

Yasmin likes the library

Yasmin liked school but the school did not offer A-Levels in Psychology and Sociology, which were the recommended subjects for Social Work.

The local tertiary college had a pleasant adult atmosphere and a mix of all ages and people on different courses. It was good to mix with a wider range of people than at school. The college also had BTEC Social Care courses, two of the staff had been social workers and regular placements existed which she could join. Yasmin had checked the examination results and had noted the well resourced library with a selection of professional journals relevant to social work on the shelves. This was for her! Yasmin chose Psychology,

Sociology and Government and Politics.

John hangs up his school uniform

John had always held a keen interest in business but he was uncertain of what particular aspect. The local college of further education attracted him as at the Open Evening he had inspected all of the computer equipment in a large, carpeted study centre. It was far beyond what the other local institutions possessed and in addition the A-Level staff also taught on the GNVQ Business Studies course and had lots of business experience. John liked the busy adult atmosphere and was glad that he could hang up his school uniform for good. He selected A-Levels in Computing, Economics and Law.

DISCUSSION POINTS

1. Which choice of school or college instinctively appeals to you and why?

2. Which school or college Open Evening was the most impressive and why?

3. What key points would you shortlist for a good A-Level course?

4. Do you think that all this competition between institutions and publication of results and HMI reports is a good thing?

2
Getting Started

The first step towards successful study is to acknowledge that you are a **student** and to begin immediately to manage your study programme.

Remember that other people in your age group will have gone straight into employment and they will be expected to work a 40 hour week every week. This means arriving promptly each morning at 8 or 9 am and not leaving for home until 5pm or later. A-Level is now your full-time job and it demands a similar commitment.

Successful study is built upon **good organisation** and your first considerations must be:

- assembling your study kit

- organising a study base

- finding motivation

- planning for study

- examining the syllabi.

ASSEMBLING YOUR STUDY KIT

To study effectively you need to possess the minimum tools of the trade. The following items are your essential shopping list:

Your essential shopping list
A4 pad of paper
Obviously you will need paper for all of your note-taking and essay writing but make sure that you buy A4 wide-lined paper with a margin. Writing on narrow-lined paper is difficult to read and leaves little space for your tutors to add comments or corrections. The pages from reporter/shorthand-style notebooks are much too small and make it impossible to judge how much you have written and are also too easily lost.

Pens etc

It is often tempting to buy an expensive pen but don't! Pens are too easily lost and ultimately cheap biros will do the same job for a fraction of the price. Instead save your money to buy:

- a ruler
- a hole punch
- an eraser
- a stapler
- a pencil sharpener
- HB pencils.

HB pencils are the recommended pencils for drawing diagrams and graphs in Maths and Science subjects.

Files

A filing system is essential for all of your subject notes and handouts. Choose one of the following:

- ring binders
- cardboard wallets.

Both are not essential to begin with so select one system as the basis of all of your filing. You will need a minimum of one ring binder or cardboard wallet per subject. The advantages and disadvantages are discussed in chapter 3.

Highlighter pens

These are useful to highlight key facts, quotes *etc* in textbooks and handouts. However, don't mark library textbooks!

Calculator

A calculator is essential for Maths and Science subjects and useful in other subjects too when calculations arise. You will need a **scientific** calculator for A-Level study. Ensure that it has a fractions button which you can recognise by the following symbol: $\boxed{A^b_c}$

Dictionary

Accurate spelling and grammar is a must for all A-Level work and so a dictionary is essential. It is worth spending money here to obtain a good, comprehensive dictionary which will include all of the specialist vocabulary you will encounter while studying A-Level.

The above study kit is sufficient to get started but you may also need to buy a textbook for each subject and other specialist items like a lab coat for Science. Your tutors will advise on any other essential requirements.

A section on 'Using study aids' in Chapter 10 advises on a range of other useful purchases to enhance your performance.

Finally, one expense you could avoid is correcting fluid. Tutors do not mind seeing your mistakes and if anything prefer to see your mistakes as it helps to identify misunderstandings. There is no need to paint out mistakes. Instead, simply cross out mistakes. Correcting fluid is also expensive, strong smelling and virtually impossible to get off your clothes or desk tops.

ORGANISING A STUDY BASE

At home you will need to study regularly and this means organising a **study base** where all of your books and files can be safely stored and where you can sit down to work.

Avoiding distractions

Think of all the distractions in the average home:

- your parents
- brothers and/or sisters
- television
- family pets
- music.

Do not fool yourself that you can study in your living room while all of the above distractions are all around you. To take in information and to concentrate fully upon a task you need peace and quiet and your study kit close at hand.

Creating space

A study base normally implies:

- a desk
- a bookcase
- drawers for files and stationery.

Realistically space is at a premium in any home and you will have to negotiate. Your bedroom is probably the best location as it is likely to be quieter than downstairs. If you share your bedroom then explain your needs to your brother or sister and come to an agreement.

Look around your bedroom and see if you can fit in a desk. If not, do you have a dressing table you could clear to use as a desk?

Find a clear wall to mount a bookcase or floor space for a freestanding bookcase. At worst clear your window sill or shelve the lower half of your wardrobe for your books.

If none of this is possible then to safeguard your books and files collect some empty cardboard boxes from your local supermarket to use for storage. Find boxes that will take A4 cardboard wallets and use them like filing cabinet drawers. A single box per subject and one for all of your study kit should keep everything well organised and easy to find. Once you have finished studying you can shunt all of the boxes out of the way under your bed.

This approach to study is important because:

- you need to be away from distractions

- your files and books need to be safe

- you must not waste time searching for basic items

- you need a proper surface for writing.

Once you organise your study base you will discover that when you sit down to study you will have an immediate sense of purpose, will be psychologically prepared and will be able to study as everything is to hand.

Finally, if it is too difficult to study at home then remember that public libraries are open at night and so are most college libraries.

FINDING MOTIVATION

AGE 25 +
Good job and comfortable salary, nice car, foreign holidays, own home, good social life.

The above tends to represent what most people want by their 20s but the big question is how to achieve it?

You might:

- win the National Lottery

- write a best selling novel

- find buried treasure

- be left a fortune by a rich relative.

Unfortunately the boring truth for most people is that they work hard and gain **qualifications**. Passing A-Level will allow you to apply for a variety of jobs with good prospects and going on to university for a degree will open up many more employment options.

Motivating yourself

Study is worthwhile but how can you find the **motivation** to study? There is no simple answer to this question because everyone is different and we all react in different ways. Some people like strict deadlines and pressure, some respond to rewards and some relate to distant goals like university or future careers. Perhaps the answer lies in all of these approaches. Consider the following:

Career goal
Identify your career goal and the qualifications and typical experience required. A career goal provides a reason for study and if you work hard there is no reason why you should not achieve it.

Future lifestyle
The material rewards given above are powerful motivators. How will you afford a house? A car? Holidays? The answer is to fulfil your career goal and obtain a good salary but first you have to pass your A-Levels!

Subject choice
Make sure that you choose subjects that really interest you. If your subjects are a chore from the start then you will never get the books out. You must gain some pleasure and satisfaction from your studies. Change subjects if necessary. This is not a problem inside the first six weeks of an A-Level course.

Study targets
A house is built brick by brick and A-Levels are passed by completing study targets week by week. Set yourself weekly study times and achievements targets each week.

Active learner
Take a pride in your studies and aim to be a subject expert. Read
ahead, watch relevant TV programmes, buy relevant magazines. You
will gain motivation by realising how much you know and understand.

The future
Reflect upon the words of Winston Churchill: 'These are your years!
Don't be content with things as they are. The earth is yours and the
fullness thereof. Enter upon your inheritance, accept your responsibilities.'

PLANNING FOR STUDY

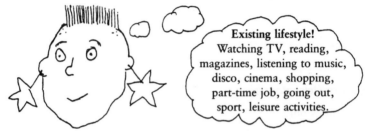

Existing lifestyle!
Watching TV, reading,
magazines, listening to music,
disco, cinema, shopping,
part-time job, going out,
sport, leisure activities.

What may be missing from your **existing** lifestyle is **studytime**. Planning
for study is very important if you are to make progress. A-Levels cover
a wealth of detail and you must absorb it slowly week by week rather
than ignoring your studies and then towards the end of your course
sitting down to a mountain of work. Your examinations may seem very
distant but it is steady work that brings success rather than last minute
cramming.

Ignoring folklore
Ignore the folklore of the brother, sister, cousin, friend who never
opened a book until two weeks before the exams and passed with a
Grade A. Such natural brilliance may be possible but if it happens at
all it is very rare. Accepting such stories is simply an excuse for not
working which you must overcome and the only certain way forward
is planning for study.
    As Churchill said, 'Accept your responsibilities'.

Identifying study times
To keep on top of A-level study you will need to put in a minimum of
two hours of work per subject, per week, on top of homework
commitments. Remember you are a student. This is your job!

You might ask why? What will I do with this time? Once you have examined the full syllabus for each of your A-Level subjects you will soon realise that your tutors only have enough time in their lessons to give a broad overview of the key topics. If you wish to gain a full understanding and especially to gain a Grade A then you will need to read around each key topic and make your own notes.

Setting study times

Find studytime for yourself by completing the **studytime planner** in Figure 1. First block out the times for:

- lessons

- travel

- meals

- favourite TV programmes

- part-time job

- sports/leisure interests

- evenings out.

Do not attempt to write in any details. Simply label and shade the relevant squares. Hopefully you can now identify times to study. Highlight two hours of studytime per subject per week. You may separate the time into two one-hour slots per subject if this is easier and often it is better for concentration. Two hours of study per subject is sufficient during your first terms but you must increase this later to meet the demands of your course.

If your commitments fill your week then you **must** reduce your commitments to ensure that you are studying weekly for your A-levels.

Finally, feel guilty every time a studytime passes and you have found excuses not to study. What did you do instead? Will it help you to pass your A-Levels? Will it help you to achieve your career goal?

Looking ahead

Forward planning is very important to know when to expect:

- subject assessments

- coursework submissions

- homework deadlines

- careers fairs

STUDYTIME PLANNER

TIME / DAY	9	10	11	12	1	2	3	4	5	6	7	8	9	10
MONDAY														
TUESDAY														
WEDNESDAY														
THURSDAY														
FRIDAY														
SATURDAY														
SUNDAY														

Fig. 1. Studytime planner.

- higher education fairs
- Oh – and holidays!

Buy a diary (preferably an academic year diary) so that you can map out the key course dates from September to July. Plan your work so that you are ready for each course demand and take charge of your studies rather than being surprised by events.

EXAMINING THE SYLLABUS

You would never consider entering a competition without first examining the rules, but you would be surprised by the number of students who take A-Level courses without bothering to check the **syllabus requirements.**

The formal Examination Board syllabus will specify:

- aims and objectives
- key topics
- examination format
- assessment schemes
- coursework details.

Your tutor will obviously explain the main requirements of the syllabus but will not be able to repeat the wealth of detail contained in the full syllabus. So be a study manager and seek out the syllabus!

Your school or college library should retain copies of every syllabus offered in the reference section. If not your tutor may be able to lend you a copy. Remember that there are eight examination boards and that a subject like History may have 14 separate options, so ensure that you select the correct syllabus. Also check that you are reading the syllabus for the summer when you are due to sit your A-Level examinations. Subjects are regularly reviewed and updated and in a subject like Literature the novels and plays are often changed.

You will not be able to take the syllabus home if it is from the reference section of the library so list the key requirements on a sheet of A4 paper as shown in Figure 2.

Subject:	Board:
Exact title:	
Key topics:	Examination:

Fig. 2. Recording syllabus topics.

A typical syllabus may involve the study of 20 to 25 key topics but it does vary significantly. Look for **key questions**. Some boards are listing key questions in the syllabus to direct your reading and thinking. They should be noted carefully.

Listing examination requirements
The methods of examination are far from standard at A-Level. Consider these random examples:

Subject	Papers	Exam %	Coursework %
Maths	2	50/50	0
Physics	2	50/35	15
History	2	35/35	30
Geography	3	30/40/15	15
English Lang	2	25/25	50
French	3	25/35/20	20
Psychology	2	40/40	20

Consequently every subject is different and it is highly important that you direct your studies towards the demands of the exams facing you. Most of the above exams are essay questions but some are multiple choice and some are practicals. The coursework is either a major part of your total marks or a minor part and may be several separate assignments or one long assignment varying from 3,000 words to 5,000 words in length.

Once you have isolated all of this information from the syllabuses please complete the summary pages in Figure 2 and place them into your relevant subject folders.

Obtaining a syllabus

You may obtain a copy of the full syllabus by writing to the publications department of the relevant Examination Board (see Useful Addresses). Request an order form and a price list as they will charge you for the syllabus. Look carefully to see if you can buy single syllabus offprints rather than paying for the full bound syllabus book.

You will notice from the order form that you can also buy copies of:

● examiners' reports

● past examination papers.

These will be useful as a part of your final revision programme and their value is discussed in Chapter 11 'Preparing for examinations'. Consequently do not buy immediately and also check to see if your library or tutors can supply copies before you do buy.

Your immediate task is simply to absorb and fully understand all of the demands of your A-Level syllabuses. No need for information overload.

CHECKLIST

Take your first steps as a study manager by:

● buying all essential stationery

● buying a good dictionary

● setting up a study base

● thinking about your career goals

● identifying weekly study times

● completing a year planner

● examining the syllabuses.

Then you can declare yourself fully prepared for study!

CASE STUDIES

Susan goes shopping

Susan strode into her bedroom with a sense of purpose after a day spent shopping in the town centre. She was loaded down with heavy bags, one full of the textbooks recommended for her subjects, the other full of general stationery items.

Susan set the bags down, pulled open the top drawer of her dressing table and cleared all of her bits and pieces off the top of the dressing table into the drawer. She pulled a large pad of A4 paper out of one of her shopping bags and placed it prominently in the centre of the dressing table. Next she laid out a row of stationery items and dropped a collection of pens and pencils into a large mug with the legend 'Student At Work' printed on the side.

One by one Susan flipped through the course textbooks before setting them on the bottom shelf of a new bookcase which was conveniently placed alongside her bed. 'Room for plenty more books,' contemplated Susan.

Satisfied with her immediate arrangements Susan retrieved *Just 17* from the bottom of the nearest carrier bag and sat down to read.

Mohammed thinks DIY

Mohammed patted the desk top and tried the drawer. 'This will do,' he said. Mr Patel pushed the trolley over which was already stacked with a flatpack bookcase and a swivel chair. The store stocked a good choice of affordable student furniture and as Mohammed was cutting back on buying CDs, videos and clothes for the month ahead it wasn't too expensive.

'Is that it?' asked Mr Patel.

'Yip, I think so,' replied Mohammed.

'Remember you're putting it all together,' laughed his father as they headed for the checkouts.

Yasmin negotiates some space

'No, you are not!'

Yasmin sighed as her younger sister Aisha pulled her bed back to its original position.

'I've got to have some room to stack books and files,' snapped Yasmin.

'Well, keep them over at your side of the room,' demanded Aisha.

'Aisha,' stated Mrs Rawat walking into the room, 'Yasmin has to have somewhere to study so let's sort this out.'

Mrs Rawat looked around the bedroom while both girls watched. She opened the cupboard and wardrobe doors and pondered.

The next half hour was all action as Mrs Rawat gave the orders and the girls cleared out the bottom of Yasmin's wardrobe and the top drawer of her chest of drawers. Shoes went under the bed along with general items.

'Files and books wardrobe,' commanded Mrs Rawat, 'and stationery top drawer.'

'There's no space for a desk,' observed Mrs Rawat, 'but you can read and make notes up here. Negotiate times with Aisha and she leaves you in peace. After 7pm when the kitchen is tidy you can write at the kitchen table.'

'Thanks, mum,' said Yasmin.

'It's a small house but with sensible discussion we can all manage.'

John finds some notes

'You bought what?'

'A desk and a swivel chair,' confirmed Mohammed.

'That's a bit OTT, isn't it?' observed John as they stood together at the bus stop.

As John sat on the bus on the way to college he thought how weird it was to buy a desk. He had always managed OK lying on the floor in front of the television and had never even considered buying a desk. He felt in his anorak pocket for his packet of mints and pulled our three crumpled sheets of paper. Notes from the first Economics lesson, he muttered and thrust them back into his pocket.

DISCUSSION POINTS

1. How does the time and effort you put into your A-Level course compare with someone you know who has a full-time job?

2. How would an employer react to someone who kept arriving late for work or taking time off without permission? Are tutors too soft? Should there be more discipline?

3. Can you say 'No' to your friends if you have homework to complete and they invite you out? Why not? Can you think of ways to say no?

4. If you fail to work hard and do not pass your A-levels what employment exists locally? What will your future hold if you seek employment with your existing qualifications?

3
Studying in the Classroom

According to the Audit Commission the time spent studying A-Level in the classroom varies from 3.6 hours up to 6.3 hours per week. This reflects the fact that there is no set tuition period for A-Level study but most students receive five hours per A-Level per week. Over the period of a two year A-Level course this adds up to a maximum of 400 hours of tuition or, taking the standard 40-hour working week as a baseline, a mere ten weeks!

It is not much time so you must take full advantage of all of your lessons by working with your tutor.

WORKING WITH YOUR TUTOR

Your tutor will have closely studied the examination board syllabus and written a **scheme of work** which spreads the teaching of the syllabus over the period of the two-year course. The scheme of work will identify all of the key topics and the order of study. Most tutors will give you a copy of the scheme of work in the first lesson but if not do ask.

The key topics from the scheme of work are your study targets and you should ensure that you work with your tutor to absorb and understand all of the topics.

First, you need to appreciate how tutors teach – see Figure 3.

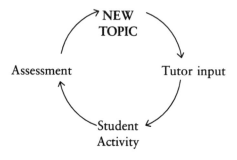

Fig. 3. The teaching cycle.

Receiving tutor input

You may expect your tutor to follow the scheme of work and introduce each new topic using a variety of different teaching methods, *eg*

- chalk and talk (or in the modern age whiteboard pen and talk)

- textbooks

- handouts

- visual aids

- video.

The purpose of tutor input is to give an overview of the topic and to guide and direct your thinking and understanding of the topic. The emphasis will be on adopting the **correct analytical approach** rather than just listing the facts or basic information. The aim is to be able to explain the facts, events, theories or reactions observed rather than merely to report them. This is analytical thinking and reasoning and it lies at the heart of A-Level work: *ie* if you witnessed a car crash you might be able to explain exactly **what** you saw (facts) but find it more difficult to explain **why** it happened (analysis).

Try to capture your tutor's analysis and guidance in your notes. Ask if you are uncertain.

Participating in student activities

To ensure that you fully understand the information most tutors will follow up their input with some form of **student activity**, *eg*:

- worked examples

- group work

- discussion

- role play

- practical

- case studies.

Tutors use these activities to make you think about the information and to explore the evidence. Student activities will also help you to develop a range of different skills like cooperating with others, listening to other opinions, sharing ideas and presenting information. These are all useful additional skills which you should consciously develop.

Completing assessments

Once a tutor has covered a key syllabus topic through a mixture of
tutor input and student activity it is crucial to measure your level of
understanding. This means **assessment!** There is no point in moving
on to the next topic if you still misunderstand the last one.
Assessments may involve:

- laboratory work

- laboratory report

- essays

- short answer questions

- multiple choice

- worksheets.

Your marks and the tutor's comments will indicate your progress.
Remember not to ignore low marks but to follow the advice given in
Chapter 10 'Reviewing your progress.'

Overall you must aim to work in parallel with your tutor and
prepare for each lesson.

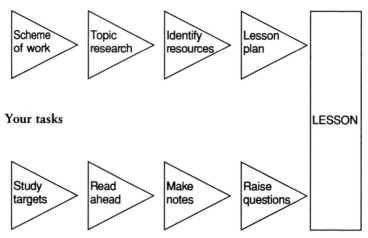

Fig. 4. Tutor and student tasks.

Accept the fact that lesson time is short and that if you wish a high grade at A-Level then this extra effort is required. If you can prepare for lessons as indicated then you will more quickly understand and absorb the key topics and be able to watch your marks and progress soar ahead.

Remember to adopt an **active** rather than a **passive** role in the classroom:

- concentrate

- ask questions

- take notes.

IDENTIFYING STUDY TARGETS

Examine the schemes of work for all of your A-Level subjects and identify the key topics listed as your **study targets**. To record your study targets rule a page as in Figure 5.

Autumn term			
Month	Subject 1	Subject 2	Subject 3

Fig. 5. Setting study targets.

The example shows columns for three subjects but please adjust to match the number of subjects you are studying.

Your task is to systematically exhaust all of the available information on each topic and to make your own notes. This is how to use the two hours of studytime per subject that you entered into your studytime planner sheet in Chapter 2.

Proceed as in Figure 6.

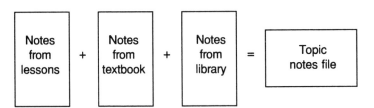

Fig. 6. Creating subject notes.

Planning for study

To complete the above work you will need to work weekly and to organise yourself carefully with a weekly planner. If you have an academic year diary then use it but otherwise draw up a study programme each week as in Figure 7.

Task	Day	Time
Read Chap Two of History textbook and make own notes	Tuesday	7 – 8 pm
Write up essay for Economics	Thursday	1 – 3pm

Fig. 7. Planning for study

Discipline yourself to work in this way and you will be on top of your work, feel more confident and gain a full understanding of each subject. This is how to achieve a Grade A. It takes this extra effort. Remember you are a student. This is your job!

Developing an academic interest

Try to take a pride in your subject knowledge. Aim to be a subject expert and it will help your motivation. Do not regard your subjects as a chore. Gain an academic interest by:

● watching relevant TV programmes

● listening to relevant radio programmes

● buying a broadsheet newspaper and clipping relevant features

● reading relevant professional magazines

● buying useful books and getting into a book-buying habit.

JOINING IN DISCUSSION AND DEBATE

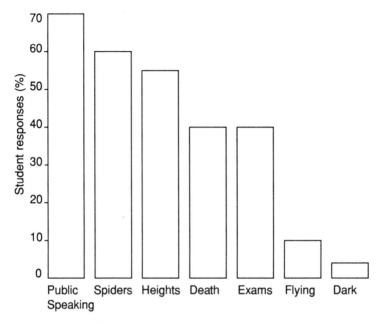

Fig. 8. A-Level students' greatest fears.

Students often rank **public speaking** above more obvious fears (see Figure 8) because no one enjoys being in the spotlight or possibly ending up looking foolish. People constantly work to improve their standard of written English but rarely practise public speaking and yet this is one of the first things other people notice about you.

Preparing a talk

No politician or public figure would dream of giving a speech which had not been carefully pre-planned and rehearsed and nor should you. The main secret of good speaking is to list all of your key points and to read and reread them until they are clear in your mind. Knowing what you want to say is the best way to relax and reduce your stress. If it is a formal presentation consider using an overhead projector. Prepare some slides with lists of your key points and some relevant illustrations. Your audience will focus their attention on the screen as you speak and it may help you to relax and act as prompt sheet for you so that you never forget where you are.

Breathing naturally

It is perfectly normal to feel nervous while waiting to speak. This is caused by your body producing extra adrenaline in response to your natural anxiety but it should melt away once you begin to speak. Simply pause if you feel nervous and catch your breath. If your mouth has a tendency to become very dry then keep a small mint in your cheek and it will maintain a flow of saliva but not impair your ability to speak.

While waiting you can help yourself to relax by practising this breathing technique:

1.   Breath in slowly through your nose.
2.   Hold it for two seconds.
3.   Exhale slowly through your mouth.

Control each breath so that you are not gasping for air and it will help you to relax.

TAKING NOTES

Note-taking is a **must**, not an option! Note-taking forces you to restate ideas or to summarise information in your own words. This is a powerful method of learning as your own words are the best guide to anything new. Open any study skills textbook and you will find page after page devoted to the merits of sequential or patterned note-taking. Don't worry about it! The best style is what works for you. Note-taking is a very personal process so do not be concerned about different methods but instead consider the following points:

Organisation
In each lesson take out a fresh sheet of A4 paper and place the date, subject and topic at the top of the sheet.

Memory
The human memory is extremely weak. Can you remember lesson details from last week? Or how about last month? So ignore classmates who do not recognise the value of taking notes. They will be wanting to borrow your notes at exam time!

Listen
Listen for the key points. Do not attempt to write down every word

but capture the explanation of a given theory or importance of a particular point.

Ask
Teaching is a two-way process so please ask if you do not understand or cannot spell a word. If you remain silent your tutor will assume that you understand and move on. Help your tutor to help you by asking questions.

Books
Record any recommended books for later study. Tutors only have time to give a broad outline. The detail and real understanding come from textbooks so follow up each topic and take notes to add to your class notes.

Make note-taking an **absolute habit** and as detailed as possible, topic by topic, as you proceed through the course. Later at exam time when the individual lessons have long departed from your memory your notes will be your only record of each topic.

FILING NOTES AND HANDOUTS

There is no point in taking notes and collecting handouts from your lessons if you cannot find them at exam time. You will not need a filing cabinet but you will need a clear **filing system**. The best systems are based upon A4 cardboard wallets or A4 ring binders. You will need to have a minimum of one ring binder or cardboard wallet per subject to start with. Once your notes begin to accumulate and you can gauge the importance of each topic you might then allocate a single file to a particular topic. The advantages and disadvantages of both methods of filing are:

	Ring binders	**Wallets**
Advantages	durable topics easily divided easy to add notes hard cover protects notes	cheap easy to carry flat/easy to store no need to punch paper

Disadvantages	expensive
	bulky to store/carry
	pages often tear out
		easily torn or bent
		difficult to find
		  information
		notes may become
		  jumbled

Adopt one system initially as the basis of all of your filing and store all of your files carefully in your study base. To avoid carrying too many files around you could use one file as your daily 'working file' and at home transfer the notes and handouts from each lesson into the relevant subject files.

CHECKLIST

Adopt good study habits by:

- reading ahead before lessons
- listing study targets for each subject
- completing a termly study planner
- completing a weekly study planner
- taking notes from lessons
- taking notes from relevant textbooks
- preparing for discussions
- creating individual subject files.

CASE STUDIES

Everyone faces the same study problems but not everyone looks for the solutions!

Susan watches *The Bill*
Susan glanced at her watch – it was 7.40 pm.

'Only 20 minutes to *The Bill*,' muttered Susan as she returned her attention to her Maths homework. She rechecked the data but something was wrong.

'Frequency bloody polygons,' said Susan as she pushed her chair away from the table and paced across the room. She lifted a tape and set it down again.

'No, no music. I promised myself *The Bill* as my reward for doing this homework.' Susan crossed the room to her bookcase and flicked through the books and extracted the Maths A-Level Study Guide she had bought at the weekend.

She searched the index for polygons and opened the book at page 24 and returned to her desk and began to read. 'Only if each triangle cut off the histogram is compensated for will the area match up with the polygon,' read Susan.

'That's it! That's it!' she exclaimed and slammed the book closed.

She reached for her calculator and worked furiously, renewing all of her data.

'Susan! *Bill*'s just starting,' came the voice of Susan's mother up the staircase.

'Just finished,' smiled Susan as she slotted her completed homework into her file.

'Well worth the money,' thought Susan as she returned the Study Guide to the bookcase and raced off downstairs.

Mohammed tapes *The Bill*

'*The Bill*'s just starting,' announced Mrs Patel.

'Can you tape it for me?' asked Mohammed, 'I'm still working on this assignment for English Language but I'll be another 20 minutes or so.'

'You could break off and complete your homework after,' suggested his mother.

'No, I'd prefer to keep it as a reward, once I've finished this,' replied Mohammed.

'Has this been any good?' asked Mrs Patel indicating the Thesaurus which was lying open on the desk top.

'Yea, it has,' confirmed Mohammed. 'I'm writing a character description and I didn't want to say "he was nice" because it sounds so weak but when you look up "nice" in the Thesaurus it gives you agreeable, amiable, attractive, charming, commendable, courteous, delightful, friendly, good, kind, likeable, pleasant, polite, refined, well mannered.'

'So what did you choose?' enquired Mrs Patel.

'I liked the sound of refined,' replied Mohammed.

'Just like your Dad,' laughed Mrs Patel as she left the room.

Yasmin watches everything

'Shouldn't you be doing some homework,' asked Mr Rawat.

'No, not Tuesday nights,' replied Yasmin as she settled down in front of the television.

Yasmin had planned out her week very carefully and had drawn up a studytime planner sheet with all of her lessons marked and with studytime hours for homework and personal study all highlighted. She managed to identify two hours for studytime on a Tuesday afternoon which kept her evening free to watch TV. She noticed that many of the other students in her class simply wasted all of the time but she had got herself into a weekly routine which worked. She felt more confident being organised and sitting down to study at the same times every week. She was able to complete all of her homework and read and take notes from textbooks and still find enough time to be with her friends.

Already in the classroom she found herself answering more and more questions and her mates were congratulating her for being so clever.

Yasmin knew that she wasn't particularly clever – she was simply sitting reading textbooks and making her own notes while they were all gossiping in the canteen. Anyone could do it!

John watches nothing in particular

John looked up at the gunfire from his position lying on the floor in front of the television. 'Not *Soldier, Soldier* again,' muttered John to himself. It wasn't a particularly favourite programme. John looked down again at his homework. He had not worked on it over the weekend as he had promised himself and it was now due. He had read the explanation of inflation twice but he still couldn't grasp it. The economics textbook was using words he had never even heard of before, so how was he meant to understand it?

'The wages, prices spiral,' read John and he groaned and closed the book and shoved it to one side. He looked up at *Soldier, Soldier* and decided to watch it after all. He'd make some excuse in class in the morning.

'How did you manage this definition of inflation?' asked John, flicking through his mate Michael's homework as they waited for the lesson to begin.

'Easy, I used this *Dictionary of Economics*,' replied Michael. 'It sets out all of the key terms and theories used in Economics and it's really easy to follow.'

'This is good too,' continued Michael, lifting up a copy of the study guide book *Mastering Economics*.

'Can I borrow these?' asked John.

'Yes, but just make sure you return them,' insisted Michael.

John took both books home and with their help soon completed his homework and decided to buy his own copies.

DISCUSSION POINTS

1. To what extent do you plan your working week or do you simply respond to demands as they arise?

2. How do you prepare for and follow up lessons?

3. If you hit a study problem do you:

   (a) seek your tutor's advice?

   (b) use textbooks and study guides?

   (c) ask a friend for help?

   (d) or ignore it?

4. Why do some students slip into a 'non-work' culture and how can you avoid it?

4
Improving Your English

> To be, or not to be: that is the question;
> Whether 'tis nobler in the mind to suffer
> The slings and arrows of outrageous fortune,
> Or to take arms against a sea of troubles,
> And by opposing end them?
>
> (Shakespeare, *Hamlet*, Act III, Scene I.)

These are perhaps the most famous words in the English language, yet Shakespeare never went to university and his first writings were not well received by the London literary establishment.

The next Shakespeare could be **you** but only if you pay attention to your standard of English and take conscious steps to improve it.

MEETING THE EXAMINERS' STANDARDS

The marking schemes for A-Level examinations do not formally specify English but most examinations include a marks section for Communications and examiners will use this section to deduct marks for poor English.

This is fair because the National Curriculum does set and formally specify the standard of English expected from Year 11 students which is *before* you enter an A-Level course.

> Grammatical features and vocabulary are accurately and effectively used. Spelling is correct, including that of complex irregular words. Work is legible and attractively presented. Paragraphing and correct punctuation are used to make the sequence of events or ideas coherent and clear to the reader.
>
> (*English in The National Curriculum*, HMSO 1995.)

Consequently A-level examiners will expect your English to be good and they often comment upon standards of English. Consider these remarks from one clearly frustrated AEB Chief Examiner in 1994:

> True understanding cannot be conveyed by badly organised, ill-spelt writing in which the recognised codes and structures of effective communication are ignored.
>
> (AEB Examination Report, 1994
> English and Communications, page 8.)

You might think this was an English examination so such opinions are to be expected, but similar concerns were also expressed by the Biology examiners:

> The examiners frequently commented on the poor standard of written English. Technical terms were poorly used . . . colloquial expression also abounded.
>
> (AEB Examination Report, 1994 Biology, page 1.)

What do examiners expect?

To answer this question put yourself in the shoes of an examiner. It is a hot day in July and you have 500 scripts to mark in a fortnight. You have marked 49 scripts and after marking the 50th you are going to stop for a cup of coffee and a rest. You lift script number 50 and discover:

✗ The answer starts halfway down the page
✗ There is no question number or title
✗ The handwriting is a scrawl
✗ Key names and terms are misspelt
✗ The punctuation is non-existent
✗ There are few or no paragraphs
✗ There are regular mistakes in grammar
✗ There is no logical progression of points.

Examiners are human! You cannot expect to pass or to gain a high grade with poor English and poor presentation. You do not have control over the questions on the examination paper but you do have control over your **standard of English**. You will delight the examiner and gain the maximum marks for Communication by:

✓ Starting all answers at the top of a fresh sheet of paper
✓ Clearly identifying the answer
✓ Correctly spelling all key words and terms associated with the subject

✓ Using basic punctuation
✓ Writing with one clear paragraph per point
✓ Avoiding dialect, slang or colloquial English
✓ Obeying rules of grammar.

The pressure of an examination and writing at speed will affect your standard of English but not to the point of excusing poor English. Improving your English should be a personal goal.

EXPANDING YOUR VOCABULARY

Studying three or more A-Levels will expose you to a much wider vocabulary than you currently possess and this process will continue once you move forward into university and employment. Every subject or job has its specialist terms which you must learn and remember and be able to spell. Can you match up the following specialist words with the right subjects:

Art	Ethnomethodology
Biology	Parapraxis
British government	Corpuscular theory
Business studies	Obligato
Chemistry	Transversality
Computing	Caveat emptor
Economics	Weltpolitik
English Language	Comminution
English Literature	Romanticism
Geography	Onomatopeia
History	Gold standard
Law	Synchronous transmission
Maths	Praseodymium
Music	Restrictive practices
Physics	Black Rod
Psychology	Rhinencephalon
Sociology	Cubism

The correct match is printed in reverse order, *ie* Cubism goes with Art, but if you want to know the meanings you will have to use a dictionary!

These specialist words are not used for the sake of using 'big' words. They are used because they convey a precise meaning and this is important the higher you progress in academic studies. Given all of the new words you will encounter at A-Level you may expect your vocabulary to leap forward as follows:

- The average five-year-old knows and uses approximately 2,000 words.

- The average 16-year-old knows and uses approximately 3,000 words.

- The average post A-Level student knows and uses approximately 20,000 words.

It is highly important to capture all of the new words you will encounter at A-Level and the best way to do this is to create your own **glossary of terms**, per subject, as in Figure 9.

Glossary of Terms	
Key word	Definition

Fig. 9. Creating a glossary of terms.

Make your glossary of terms the first page of each of your subject files and use it not only to understand the definitions but to learn the spellings. These are brand new words to you which you must learn and absorb.

CORRECTING YOUR SPELLING

Everyone has words they cannot spell but not everyone is facing an A-Level examination. You are. If your spelling is weak please make a definite effort to improve. You can improve your spelling by:

- creating a glossary of terms
- wordprocessing your work and using a spellcheck program
- carrying and using a pocket dictionary
- writing out 20 times any words you frequently misspell
- buying a spelling dictionary.

A **spelling dictionary**, available from any good bookshop, differs from a normal dictionary by listing all of the word endings. For example, if you look up the word **monopoly** the dictionary will list all of the associated words:

- monopolies
- monopolisation
- monopolise
- monopolised
- monopolising
- monopolist
- monopolistic.

This is a very useful instant reference if you are thinking, 'does that word exist?' Or do you drop the 'Y' or not? Often it is word endings that are misspelt.

Word pairs

Finally, many misspellings result from selecting the wrong word. Can you correctly match the following word pairs and definitions?

	Word pairs	*Definitions*
1.	Accept/Except	To receive_____
		To exclude_____
2.	Adopt/Adapt	To adjust_____
		To approve_____
3.	Affect/Effect	To influence_____
		A result_____
4.	Aloud/Allowed	Permitted_____
		Audible_____
5.	Already/All ready	By this time_____
		All person or things prepared_____
6.	Bare/Bear	To carry/animal_____
		Naked_____

7. Bored/Board   Make a hole/weary_____
                         Plank/receive meals_____

8. Brake/Break   To shatter/rest_____
                         To stop_____

9. Canvas/Canvass   Heavy material_____
                         Solicit votes___ _____

10. Check/Cheque   Bank order_____
                         Test/examine_____

11. Choose/chose   Present tense_____
                         Past tense_____

12. Coarse/Course   Education/racing/meal_____
                         Rough/fishing_____

13. Council/Counsel   Elected assembly_____
                         Legal adviser_____

14. Currant/Current   Existing/flow_____
                         Small berry_____

15. Desert/Dessert   Barren place_____
                         Sweet course_____

16. Disinterested/   No interest or concern_____
    Uninterested   Neutral/Unbiased_____

17. Emigrant/immigrant   Person leaving_____
                         Person entering_____

18. Formally/Formerly   Previously_____
                         Manner/approach_____

19. Hoard/Horde   Store_____
                                Crowd_____

20. Idle/Idol   Object of worship_____
                                Lazy_____

21. Loose/Lose   Not tight_____
                                Fail to win_____

22. Meter/Metre   Measure_____
                                Gas/electric_____

23. New/Knew   Not old_____
                                Past tense of To Know_____

24. Peace/Piece   A part of_____
                                No war_____

25. Pray/Prey   To worship_____
                                Hunted animal_____

26. Principal/Principle   Code of conduct_____
                                Very important/headteacher_____

27. Sew/Sow   With a needle_____
                                Plant seeds_____

28. Stationery/Stationary   Not moving_____
                                Writing materials_____

29. Waist/waste   Part of the body_____
                                Rubbish_____

30. Weather/Whether   If/possibility_____
                                Sunshine/rain_____

Hopefully you have correctly distinguished between all 30 word pairs. If you are uncertain note that the correct answers appear in the following sequence:

Odd numbers   – Word one matches definition one
              – Word two matches definition two.
Even numbers – Word one matches definition two
              – Word two matches definition one.

Try to ensure that you spell what you mean and check spellings in a dictionary if you are uncertain. There are three major publishers of dictionaries:

- Oxford

- Collins

- Chambers.

They all produce a very similar product but do look out for combined **Dictionary/Thesaurus** versions as these are normally very cost effective.

CHECKING YOUR ENGLISH

English is a living language. Every year new words appear and become a part of everyday speech and usage, *eg*:

- Virtual reality

- CD Rom

- Internet

- Eurosceptic

- Ghetto blaster

- Passive smoking

- Yuppie

- Glasnost.

Can you think of some other examples?
Similarly some words disappear from the language as students of Shakespeare and Chaucer will know, *eg*:

ballow	(cudgel)
mow	(grimace)
candied	(pampered)
chariest	(modest)
palsy	(weakness)
surtout	(overcoat)
threaped	(quarrelled)

Are you aware of any other examples?

You may also notice as you move from one region of Britain to the next that words and terms peculiar to one local area also exist. These different **dialects** along with the differences in regional accents emphasise the richness and variety of the English language. Can you think of words or phrases peculiar to one region of Britain? Can you identify someone's birthplace from their accent and particular words or phrases they use?

Many people also use **colloquial** English, which basically means using everyday speech in writing when more formal academic language should be used:

- he was in real trouble

- they had a slanging match

- they were over the moon

- over the top

- a piece of cake.

To cope with all of these variations in language it is important that everyone writes in **Standard** English. This means that written English should obey the national Standard for English which is set out in the National Curriculum, *ie* avoiding colloquial English, dialect English and using correct punctuation and grammar.

Using punctuation

Without punctuation marks your writing would simply be a jumble of words. Punctuation allows your words to be ordered into separate intelligible thoughts. Here are the basic punctuation marks in regular use:

? . ! ; ' ( ) - : ' ' " " ,

Can you punctuate the following passage making use of some of the above punctuation marks?

how good is your punctuation using punctuation marks will help you to write in clear english the alternative is

confusion
misunderstandings
loss of meaning

get it right poor punctuation like poor grammar reflects badly on you the book starting english quotes john wilson as stating writing without punctuation is anarchy but whether you agree or not try to obey the rules its your responsibility so if in doubt use a students guide

If you found the above task difficult then do take action to improve. The rules are easy to understand so please ask your tutor for help or buy a simple guide to good English.

Considering grammar

Few people possess perfect grammar but like punctuation good grammar is essential to writing clear English. Writing involves using eight different parts of speech:

1. Noun   – names of people, things, animals
2. Pronoun   – substitute for a noun, *eg* it, he, she, them
3. Verb   – doing words, *eg* running, writing, making
4. Adjective   – descriptive words, *eg* beautiful, large, funny
5. Adverb   – words which add to a verb, *eg* soon, clearly
6. Conjunction   – joining words, *eg* but, and, so
7. Preposition   – relationship words, *eg* on, under, with, above
8. Exclamation   – expressive words, *eg* Ouch! Help!

Grammar rules explain how to order and use these different parts of speech to ensure clear English and to reduce ambiguity. Grammar can be complex but if you find it difficult then be positive and seek help.

Seeking help

All A-Level tutors have a duty to promote Standard English and should correct any mistakes in grammar and punctuation when marking your work. Try to act on any mistakes identified:

- ask if you are uncertain
- list any misspellings and learn the correct spellings
- recognise and avoid dialect or colloquial English
- check punctuation rules
- correct poor grammar.

There are a number of study guides and books to help you to improve your understanding of Standard English. Look for:

- Combined dictionaries and grammar guides
- English study guides.

Check if your school or college has an **English Workshop** for extra support but if not most tutors will be willing to explain how to improve. The key is to ask and to take positive action rather than ignoring the mistakes circled in your homework.

PRESENTING YOUR WORK

There is no marks scheme for 'neatness', but untidy work has an unfortunate psychological impact on most tutors – meaning that they assume it is poor before they even read a word. **Good presentation** says that you care about your work, so please present all of your routine homework and classwork as follows:

- use A4 wide-lined paper with a wide margin unless otherwise directed
- start at the top of a fresh sheet of paper
- print the title in block capitals
- write in clear paragraphs: one paragraph per separate point
- check all spellings and especially new specialist words or terms
- highlight any quotations by placing on a separate line in quotation marks
- identify the source of any quotations in brackets
- impress by listing all of the books consulted in a bibliography
- wordprocess and use a spellcheck where possible.

This approach to all of your work will significantly enhance the appearance of your work and impress your tutor – and impressing your tutor or examiner is certainly the way to gain high marks.

Two things to avoid are:

- Correction fluid – tutors prefer to see your mistakes so there is no need to paint them out. Simply cross out any mistakes.

- Plastic sleeves – a pile of classwork in plastic sleeves slips and slides all over the place and it is a nightmare for your tutor to extract and return your work to the sleeve.

Overall good English is a reasonable expectation from an A-Level student and poor English will certainly cost you marks, so take care to improve your English.

CHECKLIST

Improve your English by:

- creating a glossary of terms for all new subject words
- learning the spelling of new words
- checking all spellings in a dictionary
- correctly using all 30 pair words
- taking care to write in **Standard** English
- buying study guides to punctuation and grammar
- presenting all work neatly and professionally
- using a wordprocessor where possible.

CASE STUDIES

Susan protests

'Your work is accurate but spoilt by not paying enough attention to presentation,' read Susan as she scanned her homework. 'Sixty-six per cent.'

'This isn't fair,' protested Susan as her Biology tutor passed between the benches returning everyone's homework.

'Why is it not fair?' enquired her tutor, stopping by her bench.

'I've used all of the headings you specified and showed us on the board,' complained Susan.

'You may have, but look at your layout,' prompted her tutor. 'Your subheadings are in lower case and buried in each line of text. They need to be printed and with a line of clear space below so that each section of your lab report stands out. Your numbering system for each paragraph is there but the numbers are again hidden by text. Present them in a clear column so that each separate paragraph can be identified. Lab reports are formal documents. They are very different from essays. Anyone checking your data or results must be able to see the relevant sections at a glance rather than scanning through all of the text. I only deducted four per cent but it was a crucial four per cent as it denies you a Grade A.'

'It just doesn't seem that big a mistake,' said Susan.

'Imagine receiving two presents from two admirers,' laughed her tutor. 'Present 1 is a box of chocolates, unwrapped with a Post It note attached saying, Got these for you! Present 2 is an identical box of chocolates but wrapped in bright gold wrapping paper with a red and gold ribbon and a small Best Wishes card saying, With all my heart! Which present attracts you more and why?'

'OK, I give in,' laughed Susan, 'I'll wrap in future!'

Mohammed discovers spellings

Mohammed took his English Language homework back out of his file and looked again at the misspellings circled by his tutor. He wanted to be a journalist and knew that he couldn't ignore poor spelling. Mohammed opened his desk drawer and took out a sheet of paper and listed all of the misspellings:

> accomodation
> relavance
> sincerly
> simular
> bureaurocacy.

He checked the correct spellings in his dictionary and looked at his watch.

'Five minutes should do it,' thought Mohammed.

Mohammed wrote all five words across the top of the sheet of paper and then listed the correct spelling of all five words 20 times each.

'Here we go,' and he turned the paper over and wrote:

> accommodation
> relevance
> sincerely
> similar
> bureaucracy.

Yasmin finds help

'Not the apostrophe again,' groaned Yasmin as she looked at the red circles dotted down her essay. She was going to settle this once and for all during her free afternoon session at college.

Yasmin pushed open the door of the English workshop and glanced at all of the shelves of handouts and textbooks.

'There must be something about the apostrophe in here some-where,' she thought.

'May I help?' asked a tutor, who suddenly appeared by her elbow.

Fifteen minutes later Yasmin left the workshop clutching a handout which set out the rules for using the apostrophe. There were only two major rules and the tutor had taken just ten minutes to explain both and highlight the examples in the handout.

John fails to act

John knew his English was weak. His teacher at high school had always commented upon his poor English. He *was* poor at English but he had managed to get through his GCSE examinations.

He glanced again at the endless circles on his Economics essay which all highlighted mistakes in English and thrust it deep into his bag. He was poor at English and that was that!

DISCUSSION POINTS

1. Do you think that English should be a part of the formal marking scheme for A-Level? If so how many marks out of 100 would you allocate to English?

2. Why should everyone write in Standard English? Should colloquial and dialect English be allowed?

3. What study aids have you bought to help improve your English?
    eg
    (a) dictionary?

    (b) spelling dictionary?

    (c) thesaurus?

    (d) grammar guide?

    (e) punctuation guide?

    How useful are they? Would you recommend any in particular?

5
Developing Science Skills

$$E = mc^2$$

On 16 July 1945 the ultimate proof of Einstein's most famous equation was demonstrated by the explosion of the world's first atomic bomb at Alamogordo in the New Mexico Desert, America. The chief physicist Robert Oppenheimer watched in awe as the now familiar mushroom cloud rose into the sky. He quoted Krishna from the Hindu Scriptures:

> 'I am become Death, the shatterer of worlds!'
> (Clark, *The Greatest Power on Earth*, page 199,
> Sidgwick and Jackson)

CONSIDERING SCIENCE SKILLS

Science is not always so dramatic but it does have the capacity to alter the world we live in and all of its arises from the basic skills of:

- observation
- hypothesis
- investigation.

The strict deployment of these skills has resulted in many scientific advances but not all in the direct line of research:

Direct research	Indirect research
1910 Bisto gravy	1896 Radiation
1915 Processed cheese	1913 Stainless steel
1926 Aerosol	1927 Nylon
1972 Calculator	1932 Soya meat
1938 Instant coffee	1933 Cat's eye
1943 Biro pen	1938 Teflon
1982 Camcorder	1970 Post It notes (non-stick glue)

Direct research implies setting a particular goal and conducting investigations until the product or desired result is obtained. Sometimes direct research will produce results within months, *eg* Bisto gravy, or take years, *eg* processed cheese, or a decade: camcorder. However, sometimes no result is obtained despite decades of dedicated research, *eg* cancer.

Indirect research refers to an unexpected outcome which when investigated leads to a new discovery, *eg* stainless steel – a new steel which did not rust.

In both cases direct and indirect scientific advances rely upon good observation.

Developing observation

To the scientist observation is a whole way of life! It means **enquiry** or always asking questions and seeking explanations. A simple observation can lead to research which leads to scientific advance, *eg*:

- Why did the apple fall to earth?   (Newton, Gravity, 1687)

- Why did bacteria touched by mould not grow?
  (Fleming, Penicillin, 1928)

- How was a photographic plate inside a box damaged?
  (Röntgen, X-rays, 1895)

- Why do people who do not eat fresh fruit and vegetables die?
  (Lind, Vitamins, 1758)

Try to take a full interest in your studies and develop an enquiring, active interest in science. Read *New Scientist* every week, library textbooks and watch *Horizon* on television. Look around you and question! Questions lead to hypotheses which lead to investigations in the laboratory. There is no reason why you should not go on to leave your mark in scientific history!

WORKING IN THE LABORATORY

Working in the laboratory is very different from working in a classroom due to the presence of:

- fragile apparatus

- hazardous chemicals

- experiments in progress.

Consequently you should always enter a laboratory with caution and act in a professional manner. Simple points like placing your bags where no one can trip over them are suddenly very important in a laboratory.

Learning from practicals

Practical laboratory experiments form an important part of the study of science because it is from experiments which help to prove or disprove a hypothesis that scientific knowledge is established. Consequently for scientific research to be valid and beyond dispute scientists must:

- construct a hypothesis
- plan an experiment to test the hypothesis
- conduct the test
- observe the reactions
- take accurate readings and measurements
- record all results
- infer conclusions
- prove or disprove the hypothesis
- write a full account of the investigation (laboratory report).

Classroom instruction will introduce you to the specified syllabus topics and help you to understand the theory but **practicals** will introduce you to scientific **method** and the skills of **investigation**.

Your ability to conduct investigations is a formal part of the examinations for most science A-Levels. You may expect 20 per cent of the final marks for the examination to be allocated to your ability to conduct practical laboratory investigations. Your tutor will prepare you for assessed practicals and will in particular assess your ability to:

- plan the investigation
- conduct the investigation
- take measurements
- present data
- form conclusions.

You must be able to demonstrate all of the above skills, and your ability to choose and use apparatus and take and present accurate measurements will determine your mark.

Consequently follow your tutor's guidance carefully and give laboratory work your full concentration as **accuracy** in science is an absolute requirement.

WRITING LABORATORY REPORTS

A **laboratory report**, because of the precision required, demands a very formal layout and style of writing. There can be no room for ambiguity in science. Your first consideration is to ensure that you use scientific language correctly.

Absorbing vocabulary

The lay person will have a general understanding of the following words:

● electricity

● gas

● water.

However, in Physics, Chemistry and Biology these are very imprecise terms and more exact terms need to be employed.

● In Physics **electricity** involves: electric current, electric charge, electronic charge, current density, electrical energy, electrical potential, electrical power, resistance, internal resistance, resistivity, conductivity, capacitance, time constant, relative permittivity, and vacuum *etc.*

● In Chemistry **gas** involves: helium, ideal gas, diffusion, neon, argon, plasma, effusion, methane, liquefaction, nitrogen, ammonia, kinetic energy, hydrogen, carbon dioxide *etc.*

● In Biology **water** involves: oxygen, hydrogen, colloidal state, density, solvent, thermal property, suspension, viscosity, light penetration, dissociation, osmoregulation, dehydration, polymerisation, condensation, oxidation, neutralisation, deamination *etc.*

Even everyday words have a more precise meaning when used in science, *eg* stress, passive, energy, force, resistance. Make sure that you fully understand and can use the correct terms. Develop a glossary of terms for each subject as described in Chapter 4 and invest in a subject dictionary.

Perfecting presentation

The exact style of presentation will vary from tutor to tutor but you should expect a laboratory report to include the following formal sections:

1. Title of experiment   Print in BLOCK LETTERS, underlined, at the head of a sheet of A4 paper.

2. Object or aim   State the hypothesis as an aim, *ie* a direct statement of the intention.

3. Apparatus   List all of the apparatus used and include details of its arrangement.

4. Diagrams   Draw, using an HB pencil, the apparatus illustrating the test cycle. Keep to straight line drawings, nothing elaborate and no colours unless otherwise directed. Do arrow appropriate flows.

5. Method   A step-by-step description of all actions employing a precise vocabulary as indicated above. Write in the strict third person, which means avoiding sentences which begin with 'I'. Aim for a direct record that someone else could read and duplicate.

6. Observations/ measurements   Record all readings and results using graphs and tables as appropriate.

7. Results   Write an exact account of what the data shows.

8. Discussion   Discuss the results and findings as measured against the original hypothesis. What is your conclusion?

To ensure that your laboratory report follows a step-by-step approach and that the individual parts can easily be referred to use a numbering system as follows:

     1.
     1.1
     1.2
     1.3
     2.
     2.1 *etc.*

DRAWING DIAGRAMS

All science subjects involve the ability to draw and label simple sketches. Often this simply means the arrangement of apparatus, but in Biology you will be expected to regularly draw specimens, tissue samples and plant cells.

The key requirements are neatness and accuracy:

• use good quality A4 plain drawing paper

• an HB pencil

• print and underline the title

• indicate the scale

• centre the drawing to dominate the page

• leave sufficient space for labels

• keep all labels strictly parallel to the top of the page.

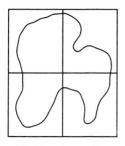

To help you draw try placing a box around the specimen as indicated and rule it into quarters (see Figure 10). If the specimen is more of an elongated shape then enclose it in a rectangle and rule it into six or eight boxes. This technique allows you to study and draw one section at a time.

Fig. 10. Drawing a diagram

Connect your labels to the relevant part by ruling straight pencil lines. These are called leader lines. To avoid confusion please ensure that none of your 'leader lines' crosses another. It is also normal practice, unless otherwise directed, to include a **brief annotation** beneath each label, which simply means highlighting or defining more closely the relevant part.

Overall, keep your diagrams and sketches simple and avoid clutter.

USING GRAPHS AND TABLES

Candidates are expected to maintain a good standard of presentation in graphs, diagrams, tables and also in the description of experimental work.

(AEB Physics Syllabus 1995)

A similar direction exists for Biology and Chemistry and it serves to underline the importance of graphs and tables in science.

The following brief notes indicate the main methods of displaying data which you must become very familiar with. A detailed account of how to use and display statistics is given in Chapter 6.

Presenting tables

RAINFALL (MM)				
MONTH	1992	1993	1994	1994

Fig. 11. Drawing a table.

Ensure that all tables are neatly ruled with the headings in BLOCK LETTERS and the unit of measurement clearly shown. Vertical columns of figures are the accepted convention rather than horizontal. Rule the border of your table with a thick line and use thin lines for the internal divisions. Neatness is the key!

Choosing graphs

The data recorded in a table may be best appreciated and understood if presented as a graph. A graph allows the eye to immediately take in comparisons and trends at a glance. You should become famUar with the forms of graphical presentation as shown in Figure 12 and choose the form which best suits the data to be displayed.

CHECKLIST

Develop your science skills by:

- taking an active interest in science
- observing laboratory health and safety rules
- conducting practicals as directed
- using all instruments and apparatus correctly
- taking accurate measurements
- creating a glossary of terms
- writing laboratory reports using formal subsections
- drawing accurate diagrams and sketches
- presenting data in graphs and tables.

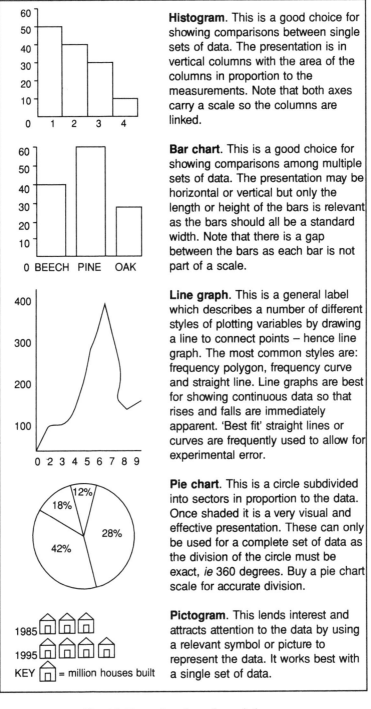

Histogram. This is a good choice for showing comparisons between single sets of data. The presentation is in vertical columns with the area of the columns in proportion to the measurements. Note that both axes carry a scale so the columns are linked.

Bar chart. This is a good choice for showing comparisons among multiple sets of data. The presentation may be horizontal or vertical but only the length or height of the bars is relevant as the bars should all be a standard width. Note that there is a gap between the bars as each bar is not part of a scale.

Line graph. This is a general label which describes a number of different styles of plotting variables by drawing a line to connect points – hence line graph. The most common styles are: frequency polygon, frequency curve and straight line. Line graphs are best for showing continuous data so that rises and falls are immediately apparent. 'Best fit' straight lines or curves are frequently used to allow for experimental error.

Pie chart. This is a circle subdivided into sectors in proportion to the data. Once shaded it is a very visual and effective presentation. These can only be used for a complete set of data as the division of the circle must be exact, *ie* 360 degrees. Buy a pie chart scale for accurate division.

Pictogram. This lends interest and attracts attention to the data by using a relevant symbol or picture to represent the data. It works best with a single set of data.

Fig. 12. Examples of graphs and charts.

CASE STUDIES

Of our regular set of case studies only Susan takes science so please follow her progress and some examples of scientific discovery.

Susan measures pollen

Susan stared down the microscope at the slide of pollen grains but even with the microscope she could only just make them out. She had sketched one as directed but how to measure one? 'Apply last week's lesson on the micrometer,' hinted the tutor as he circulated around the room. Susan returned to the notes she had taken on the micrometer and within minutes she had found the answer. As her classmates watched, Susan used a micrometer to measure the diameter of a thin length of wire and placed it under the microscope and used the wire as a base measurement to calculate the pollen size. She had forgotten the information about the micrometer after only a week but her detailed notes provided the answer.

Why do milkmaids not catch smallpox?

In 1796 Edward Jenner observed that milkmaids who had caught cowpox did not catch smallpox. This led him to a hypothesis. Does cowpox protect against smallpox? After some practical investigation using fluid taken from cowpox blisters Jenner was able to demonstrate that patients given the fluid did not develop smallpox. The body produced antibodies in response to the mild cowpox infection which attacked and killed the smallpox virus. Jenner named his treatment a vaccine and today there are many vaccines against many viruses. Smallpox was a big killer with over 600,000 cases in 1950 prompting a health campaign to eradicate it. This worldwide war against smallpox succeeded and in 1980 the virus was declared extinct. It now only exists under strict security in some university science laboratories. All of this began with just good observation and a simple hypothesis.

Where did the colour red come from?

In 1856 William Perkins was busy conducting experiments on coal tar in the Royal College of Chemistry in London. He was trying to find a source of quinine when unexpectedly some of his samples of coal tar turned red. After further investigation Perkins was able to produce a rich mauve colour. He had created the world's first artificial dye and within two years all of the colours of the rainbow were generated from the chemical base of coal tar and vegetable dyes became history. The Germans took up this British invention, which was largely ignored in Britain, and within a few years had established a world lead in dye manufacture. This was a good example of indirect research when an unexpected result leads to a positive discovery.

How can you prevent carbon from burning?

In the 1870s the principles of electric light were understood. If electric current flows along a thin filament of carbon the carbon will glow white hot and produce a bright light but the problem was that the carbon soon burned away. On 18 December 1878 Sir Joseph Swan demonstrated the solution to a meeting of the Newcastle-Upon-Tyne Chemical Society. After years of direct research he was able to create a vacuum inside the light bulb and this prevented the carbon from burning. Electric light was a reality and the first practical result came in 1880 when Swan's house, No 99 Kells Lane, Gateshead, became the first house in England to have electric light instead of gas.

Over in American Thomas Edison obtained similar parallel results but as he was the first to file a patent it is he and not Swan who is recorded by history as the father of electric light.

DISCUSSION POINTS

1. What, in your opinion, are the most significant advances in science this century? You might consider the fields of:

    (a) medicine

    (b) communication

    (c) transport

    (d) food

    (e) electronics

    (f) energy.

2. Considering the quotation from Robert Oppenheimer (page 64) do you think scientists have a moral responsibility? Is it possible to control scientific knowledge?

3. How would you defend the funding of indirect scientific research?

6
Working with Statistics

In Lordship 2 ploughs; 5 slaves; 7 villagers and
6 smallholders with 6 ploughs. Woodland 30 acres,
pasture 2 leagues, 104 unbroken mares, 25 cattle,
8 pigs, 100 sheep and 30 goats.

This is the entry for the village of Brendon, Devonshire as recorded in the Domesday Book 1086. The Domesday Book is the earliest example of official statistics in British history when King William I ordered a complete record of all 13,000 settlements in England so that he could calculate the national income and more importantly the taxes due to him.

The next significant collation of national statistics was not until 1801, when the first census was undertaken, and ever since statistics have become a way of life. Virtually every aspect of life comes down to a line graph and so it is important to be able to work with statistics. There is literacy and numeracy so why not graphicacy!

CONSIDERING SKILLS

All or some of the following skills will be demanded of you according to the A-Level subjects you have chosen to study:

- calculate
- compile
- tabulate
- draw graphs
- draw charts
- read
- interpret.

Students of Maths, Sciences, Economics and Psychology will find it necessary to develop all of the above skills, whereas the students of most Humanities subjects will only be required to read and interpret statistics. The syllabus for your subjects will specify the extent to which you must display competency in statistics.

COMPILING STATISTICS

There are two types of data: **primary** and **secondary**. Primary data are original data compiled from laboratory investigations, interviews, surveys, questionnaires and field work. Secondary data are all published data from official sources, textbooks or magazines.

Generating primary data

The study of subjects like Psychology, Sociology, Economics, Geography, Geology and the sciences often involves generating and using primary data. In the case of science subjects, Geography and Geology data arise naturally in the course of laboratory work or fieldwork and you will be expected to tabulate and present this data in the form of graphs. Science deals with **quantitative** data, *ie* numbers and values, and so accuracy and reliability are rarely issues.

Social Science research can be more complex due to the nature of Social Science enquiry, *eg*:

- How many shoppers use the shopping centre?

- How do the shoppers divide according to social class?

- What facilities do the shoppers expect/want in the shopping centre?

These are very simple questions but arriving at the answers raises many problems:

- How can you count or estimate the number of shoppers?

- Will the numbers of shoppers vary according to the time of day?

- How can you define someone's social class?

- Will pensioners, the disabled and parents with children all identify different needs?

This is qualitative data, *ie* descriptive, named data, and here there is often an issue of reliability and validity. Social Science students investigate all of the techniques of social enquiry with a particular emphasis on what is meant by reliability and validity.

Finding secondary data

A host of government agencies principally the Central Statistical Office, and numerous commercial organisations and publications compile statistics on every conceivable aspect of national life.

Look in the reference section of your library and you will hopefully find:

Central Statistical Office
Annual Abstract of Statistics. Offers statistics on population, government departments, courts, education, employment, industry *etc.*
UK National Accounts. Financial data on all aspects of government.
Business Monitor. Statistics on all aspects of industry and business.
Regional trends. Statistics on social trends with full UK regional breakdowns.
Family spending. Covers all aspects of family finance and living standards.
Social trends. Details of consumer spending and social change.

Office of Population Censuses and Surveys
Population Trends. All aspects of population data from the census and related surveys.

HMSO
Britain 1995 etc. An annual volume charting official trends and developments in Britain. Look for back copies as well as the current volume.

The Statesman's Yearbook
Annual volume of general information about world organisations, and foreign countries.

Whitakers Almanac
Annual volume covering general developments in British government, media, industry etc.

Hutchinson/Gallup Info 1995
An annual volume covering all aspects of national life with the added bonus of topical Gallup survey information at the end of each section.

All of these statistics are very informative both as immediate sources of information for subjects like Sociology and Economics and as examples of professional presentation.

PRESENTING STATISTICS

It is often said that a picture is worth a thousand words but in the world of numbers a graph is worth a thousand figures. Graphs and charts are **highly visual** and this is their strength and something you must maintain whenever you present statistics.

Choosing a layout

The aim is for your graph or chart to dominate a standard A4 sheet of graph paper with sufficient space for the scale and the labels to be entered. You may present your graph in one of four main layouts (see Figure 13).

The 2 x 3 portrait tends to be the most common style of graph, but study the range of the X and Y variables and decide which layout would best suit the data.

Presenting your graph

Aim for a clear presentation of your graph as follows:

- PRINT a title parallel to the top of the page

- PRINT labels on both axes parallel to the axis

- Place the appropriate units of measurement in brackets.

The vertical axis of a graph is the **ordinate** or **Y** axis and the horizontal axis is the **abscissa** or **X** axis. The point where both axes meet is the **origin** or more simply just 0. Select a scale for your Y and X axes which is just greater than the data range to be plotted and take care to adopt manageable units. This means counting the squares available on each axis and adopting a scale which bests fits the data. Adjust the scale if necessary to obtain a good visual rise or fall of data as this is the whole point of graphs.

Using graphs and charts

Students of A-Level Mathematics, Sciences, Economics, Psychology and Statistics in particular may encounter some specialist graph forms:

- frequency polygon

- frequency curves

- strata charts

- semi-logarithmetic graph

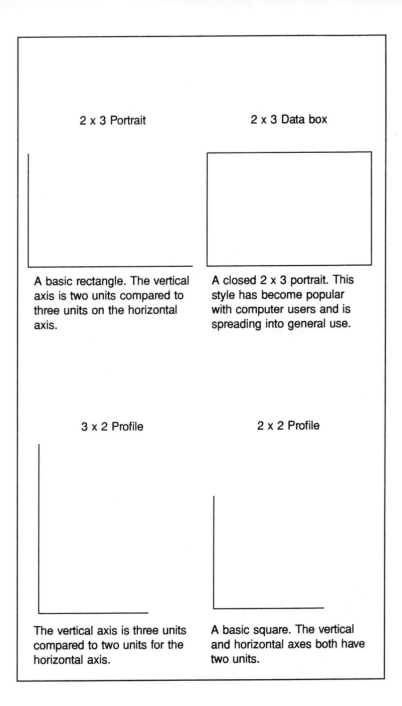

2 x 3 Portrait

A basic rectangle. The vertical axis is two units compared to three units on the horizontal axis.

2 x 3 Data box

A closed 2 x 3 portrait. This style has become popular with computer users and is spreading into general use.

3 x 2 Profile

The vertical axis is three units compared to two units for the horizontal axis.

2 x 2 Profile

A basic square. The vertical and horizontal axes both have two units.

Fig. 13. Examples of graph layouts.

- Gantt chart
- Break-even chart
- Z Chart
- Lorenz curve
- Scatter graph.

This will mean close involvement with statistical analysis, *eg* correlation, normal distribution, standard error, probability, variance.

The more general forms of graphical presentation which all A-Level students should be familiar with are as follows:

- Line graph
- Bar chart
- Histogram
- Pie chart
- Pictogram.

Please ensure that you can draw and use the above set of graphs and charts to present statistics. This will be an examination requirement for many students and an important basic skill for everyone else.

Using a line graph

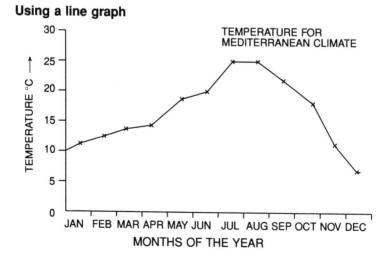

Fig. 14. Example of a line graph.

Select a line graph when you wish to show a rise or fall in data over time or particularly in science to plot measurements and variables. This means having two sets of quantitative data to plot, *ie* numbers or time scales. If one of your sets of data is qualitative, *ie* a descriptive label, a bar chart may be best. Note that the line is called a **data curve** even when it is straight.

Using a bar chart

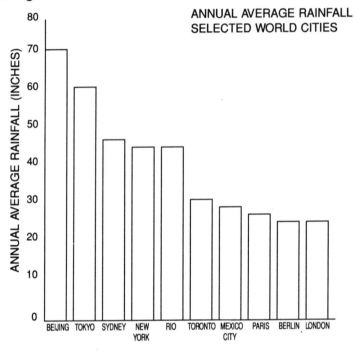

Fig. 15. Example of a bar chart.

A bar chart is very quick and easy to draw. Select it for displaying a given quality or description against a variable, *ie* names of objects, places or events. Place the unit of measurement on the Y axis and the relevant labels on the X axis. In the above example it is cities. To plot the data simply raise vertical bars as shown above. The bars should all be a standard width as the X axis does not carry a scale. Maintain a gap between the bars and note that it may be presented vertically or horizontally.

Using a histogram

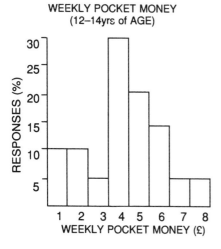

This looks like a bar chart but is not so take care not to confuse the two. Select a histogram when the data for the X axis is in the form of a scale, *eg* times, months, measurements. The variables on the Y axis will indicate the frequency, but in both cases the data is quantitative and this is the significant difference from a bar chart.

Fig. 16. Example of a histogram.

Using a pie chart

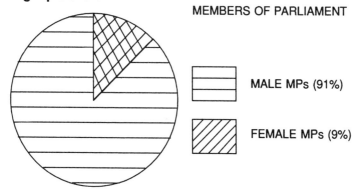

Fig. 17. Example of a pie chart.

A pie chart is very effective at capturing attention because of its shape. Select a pie chart when you have a complete set of quantitative data listing the divisions of a whole. You cannot leave a slice of your pie blank! It all has to be accounted for so that the eye can compare each data division as a proportion of the whole. Stationery shops sell pie chart scales which mark all the sectors of a circle so plotting your data is very easy. Go out and buy one today!

Using a pictogram

TOP CHAMPAGNE IMPORTERS

Germany

Britain

USA

Switzerland

Italy

Japan

Key: one glass represents one million bottles imported.

Fig. 18. Example of a pictogram.

Pictograms are a good visual variation on a bar chart as the qualitative data is represented by a relevant drawing, *eg* champagne glass for champagne. They are quite popular in magazines and newspapers but care must be taken not to mislead. To ensure accuracy it is best to adopt a standard size drawing as representative of a given value, *eg* one glass equals one million bottles as above.

READING GRAPHS AND CHARTS

All of us frequently glance at graphs and charts in our daily newspapers and in textbooks but do we actually read them?

To read the data you must:

- Discover **who produced the data**. Independent sources like Gallup or an academic researcher? Possibly biased sources like a commercial company or a pressure group?

- Check the **title**. What precisely is being shown?

- Check the **labels** for the measurement or scale in use.

- Find the **sample size**. How many respondents stated this?

- How was the sample selected? **Who took part** in the survey?

- Compare with **previous results**. What were last year's figures?

- Question the term **average**. Would the median or mode be better?

Means, modes and median

Most people are familiar with the term average or more correctly the **mean** but cannot apply the **mode** or **median**. Both are useful calculations to check against the mean:

- Mode – the most frequent response in any set of data

- Median – the midpoint of a frequency distribution once placed into rank order.

A few very high or low values may distort the mean and make it unrepresentative of the overall responses. The mode may be used to isolate any peaks or troughs in a frequency response. The median allows the position of individual scores to be judged against the middle value of the rank order. It is often useful to know if a response is in the top quarter or the bottom quarter *etc.*

Deciding which to use
The manager of a local branch of McDonald's selects 15 customers at random and records their ages as follows:

48, 10, 26, 65, 16, 17, 7, 36, 16, 75, 15, 12, 60, 34, 16

The sum total of all of the ages is 453 which, when divided by the 15 respondents, gives a mean age of 30.2.

Can the manager safely conclude that the average age of a McDonald's customer is 30? The median and mode may be more useful in this situation. First list all of the ages in rank order from the oldest person to the youngest person. The median is the middle point of the data, which in this example is 17 years. If you had an even number of respondents the median would be calculated by adding the middle two years and dividing by two. The mode is the most frequent response and here it is age 16. Is this more realistic? Consequently always consider the mode and median when examining data.

Final word

Let's give the final word in this consideration of statistics to Benjamin Disraeli, Prime Minister of Britain 1868 and 1874–80:

There are three kinds of lies: lies, damn lies, and statistics.

This is perhaps unfair but Disraeli was a politician and maybe this was an early soundbite!

Statistics, even if questionable, give everyone a common base-point in discussion and aid decision making. Look back at the bar chart on rainfall. How does the evidence of statistics contradict the popular assumption that England has a high rainfall?

CHECKLIST

Discover how to work with statistics by:

- distinguishing between primary and secondary data
- identifying qualitative and quantitative data
- choosing a layout which best suits the data
- selecting a graph which bests suits the data
- presenting data accurately in a variety of graphs and charts
- reading and questioning data.

CASE STUDIES

All four of our case study students are in the classroom learning more about statistics.

Susan works it out!

Susan looked again at the table of data she had collated from the textbook entitled *Gestation Periods of selected Mammals*.

'Number of weeks is quantitative data,' muttered Susan to herself, 'and that always goes on the Y axis.' She looked at the range of weeks to be plotted and decided that intervals of two weeks would allow the data to fill the graph.

'Mammals,' considered Susan, 'no scale involved here so it's qualitative data so a bar chart will be the best presentation.'

Mohammed stretches a percentage

'Market researchers look for the dramatic,' said Mohammed's tutor as they looked at the topic of advertising.

'In this example shampoo sales rise by 10 per cent over a six-month advertising campaign. Can you plot this rise in an eye-catching, dramatic line graph?' challenged the tutor. Mohammed started with a 'normal range' of percentage increase:

5, 10, 15, 20, 25 per cent

but noted how a 10 per cent rise on this scale looked most unimpressive. After a few minutes of experimentation Mohammed produced a sharp rise with the following scale:

2, 3, 4, 6, 10, 12 per cent

'Excellent,' confirmed his tutor, 'you have made what is a modest rise in sales look outstanding and this is one of the tricks of statistics.

The lesson is?' asked the tutor.

'Check the scales and read all graphs with care,' answered the class.

Yasmin doesn't appreciate the point

'The average family size in Britain is 2.3 children', read Yasmin from her Sociology textbook. 'It's not possible.'

'It is if you add up all of the children and divide by the number of families,' replied her tutor, 'but you might find that the mode makes more direct sense. Study the statistics given and identify the mode. Next, plot a scattergram on social class and family size and report back on any correlation.'

Yasmin looked at her completed scattergram. 'So family size does vary according to social class,' she concluded.

'That's the evidence of the data,' confirmed her tutor, 'and this is how you must use statistics to support conclusions.'

'I never saw the point of statistics before,' said Yasmin, 'but this really does prove a point.'

John finds a deficit

'Why plot figures on a line graph?' John asked his Economics tutor. 'It says here that government expenditure rises to £330 billion whereas government income only rises to £260 billion so the deficit is £70 billion.'

'Correct,' confirmed his tutor, 'but the figures do not convey to you the size of the gap between expenditure and income and especially not the variations over time. 'A line graph will highlight the gap and make the deficit more obvious.'

After half an hour John could see the importance of the graph and how easy it was to identify the size of the deficit. It did bring the figures to life.

'Graphs are all about good, effective communication,' concluded his tutor.

DISCUSSION POINTS

1. To what extent do you think Disraeli was correct?

2. Do you think that Humanities students should be expected to display competency in using statistics? Is 'graphicacy' a necessary core skill?

3. What problems do social scientists face in generating reliable and valid data?

7
Writing Essays

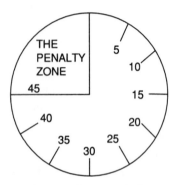

Fig. 19. The essay clock.

Writing essays to A-Level standard is mainly all about time. In a typical A-Level examination you will only have 45 minutes in which to plan and write an essay. If you stray into the penalty zone you will take time away from your later answers and end up rushing or not completing your final essay. This is a significant test of ability but it is actually manageable and relatively easy once you adopt a step-by-step approach.

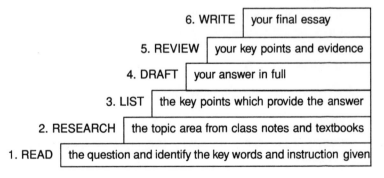

Fig. 20. Steps to essay success.

READING THE QUESTION

Candidates need to attend to the precise wording of the questions.

This advice given by an AEB Chief Examiner in 1995 picks up one of the most common reasons for failure and under-achievement in A-Level examinations. Too many candidates seize on the topic of the question rather than the key words and the instruction given.

Look at this example:

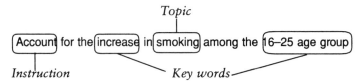

In the stress of an examination many candidates will just lock onto the topic of smoking and pour out everything they were taught about the subject of smoking and the tobacco industry, *eg*:

- tobacco cultivation techniques
- major tobacco growers
- tobacco companies
- cigarette manufacture
- distribution and warehousing
- retail sales
- tax policy
- promotion and advertising
- medical concerns
- smoking trends.

No essay title ever states: Tell me everything you know about subject X. You must discipline yourself to look beyond the topic and identify the instruction and the key words. The instruction will set the direction of your answer and the key words will set particular considerations or dates to stay within. In the above example only the sub-topic 'smoking trends' is relevant and within that only the 16–25 age group. The rest of the information may be related to smoking but it is all entirely irrelevant – no matter how well you know and remember it! The examiner will not admire your detailed knowledge of the subject of the tobacco industry but will only credit the information directly relevant to the set question.

Identifying the instruction

A variety of **instruction words** are used in A-Level examination questions:

Instruction	*Meaning*
account	explain, give reasons why
analyse	identify and discuss explanations
assess	consider, weigh up, judge, offer opinion
compare	find similarities and differences
contrast	discuss differences
criticise	express opinions, agreement, disagreement
define	give precise, detailed meaning
discuss	cover views for and against, argue opinion
describe	give complete overview
evaluate	weigh up, judge explanations, summarise
examine	investigate, consider flaws in argument
explain	provide clear reasons why
how far	judge against other explanations
indicate	list, describe explanations
illustrate	clarify with examples
interpret	translate into clearer meaning
judge	consider and rule on significance
justify	defend an explanation
outline	list and describe main points
state	precise, clear summary
summarise	identify and present main points
to what extent	level of agreement, points for and against
trace	link chain of events.

The instruction words are there to be obeyed and should set the direction of your writing. Ensure that you reflect the instruction words in your essay planning and essay structure. Check past examination papers to see which instruction words are regularly favoured by the examiners for your subjects and absorb the meanings and the style expected.

Likewise closely observe and keep to the key words which define the scope of the question. Remember that your examiners will have carefully chosen the words of the essay title to force you to consider one aspect of a topic – not the entire topic. Stop and study the question: Think **instruction** and **key words**.

IDENTIFYING KEY POINTS

Once you have isolated the instruction and the key words from an essay title you must ensure that you adopt an analytical approach by identifying the **key points** which answer the question. Your lesson notes will be an immediate source of information but you should also use library textbooks to obtain extra details and some evidence to support your choice of points, *eg* relevant statistics, quotations, opinions of leading writers. If you were to research the essay title on smoking given as an example earlier, you might identify the following points to explain the increase in smoking in the 16–25 age group:

- pleasing image

- peer group pressure

- addiction

- power of advertising

- pleasure

- rebellion statement.

These points represent an **analysis** of the question. To analyse simply means to break something down into parts and this is the approach demanded at A-Level. Do not write until you are satisfied with your key points. Try saying them aloud (in the privacy of your bedroom). Do they sound convincing? If you were engaged in debate are they firm, clear points you could defend? Check your key points against the essay question to ensure that you are obeying the instruction and the key words. Finally, decide the best **order of presentation** of your key points and number them. You are now ready to write the first draft of your essay.

DRAFTING THE ESSAY

An A-Level standard essay is a minimum of 750 words or three sides of A4 paper in average handwriting and a maximum of 1,000 words or four sides of A4 paper. To fall beneath this standard will affect your marks and to go above simply eats away your time and places

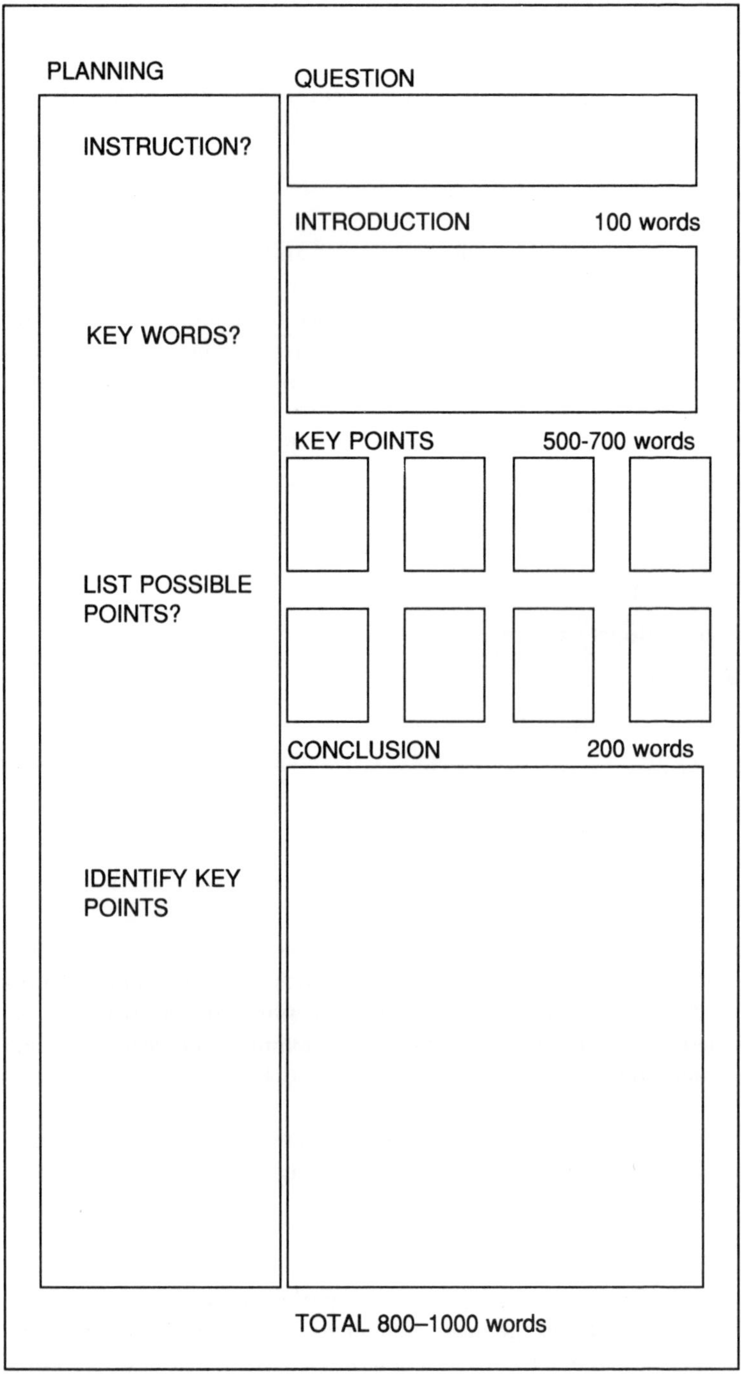

Fig. 21. Essay planner.

you into the 'penalty zone'. The law of diminishing returns also applies to a long essay. This may seem daunting but remember that you have two years to reach this standard and that an essay is easy to write once you subdivide it into the following distinct sections:

Introduction
Regard 100 words or a third of a side of A4 paper as your absolute maximum introduction. If anything keep to around 70 words or only three or four sentences. Pick up the key words from the question and follow the direction set by the instruction word(s). Avoid lengthy background information and keep exactly to the terms of the question.

Main text
Identify six to eight key points which provide a good answer to the question set and write a paragraph around each point as follows:

Link the point to the question.
Describe the relevant event, theory, opinion.
Support with evidence and discussion.
Connect to the next paragraph.

Adopt this approach paragraph by paragraph so that it all flows as one continuous piece of writing. You might write 500 to 700 words or at least two sides of A4 paper.

Conclusion
The conclusion must be a concise summary of your key points and evaluate your evidence and key points. If you introduced six key reasons/explanations as your answer which one or two points do you regard as most significant? Finish by giving a direct answer to the question set. Aim to write 200 words maximum or at least half a side of A4 paper: 130 words.

Make use of the essay planner sheet in Figure 21 to plan your essays. Reproduce this layout on an A4 page. Ask your tutor to check your plan before writing up the essay.

Adopting the correct style
Few students immediately write a perfect essay. It takes regular practice and often the most difficult part is writing in an analytical style rather than a factual or a descriptive style. You can help yourself to develop an **analytical writing style** by:

Writing in the third person
This means never starting a sentence with:

- I think . . . .
- I feel . . . .
- I believe . . . .

The correct approach is to let the evidence speak! Remain neutral and review the available evidence and explain the theories/opinions of key writers as discussed in lessons and textbooks. You can keep to the third person by starting sentences like:

- The evidence points to . . . .
- It would appear that . . . .
- It is possible to . . . .
- X has indicated that . . . . *etc.*

Argument
In all of your writing and note-taking try to distinguish between:

What happened *ie* the facts/description of a given theory/event

and

Why it happened *ie* how the theory applies.

All A-Level topics will introduce you to a range of opinions and theories and it is your task to steer your reader through all of the explanations and in so doing demonstrate your own understanding of the significance and importance of the information.

REVIEWING AND WRITING

Once you have written a full draft of your essay walk away from it. No one gets an essay absolutely right first time. Take a few hours' break or better still one or two days and then review what you have written.
Read and look for:

- an introduction which directly picks up the question

- a clear paragraph per point

- a link between each point and the question

- evidence which supports each point

- a conclusion which evaluates as well as summarises

- good English, *ie* grammar, punctuation and spelling.

Above all make sure that your essay flows from start to finish. Add further linking sentences if need be to ensure that all of your paragraphs are interlinked and lead to a complete answer to the question.

Alter your draft as necessary, give it a final 'polish' and rewrite it carefully.

This task will be much easer if you wordprocessed your essay as it is a simple matter to delete and add text on a wordprocessor. A study in the *Psychology Review* magazine (November 1995) reports that wordprocessors can significantly improve the writing ability of less able writers, so make use of your college/school equipment. Some universities are already allowing wordprocessors into examinations.

CHECKLIST

Aim to write Grade A standard essays by:

- reading the question carefully
- obeying the instruction and key words
- listing the key points
- using the essay planner sheet
- keeping the introduction concise
- writing a clear paragraph per point
- providing a conclusion which evaluates the evidence
- checking your use of English
- practising writing essays to a strict 45-minute time limit.

CASE STUDIES

Susan stops thinking

'Look at this sentence,' instructed Susan's tutor as he returned her homework. 'You've written: I think the rise in temperature was important because I observed that the liquid began to boil.'

'Correct,' replied Susan.

'The information may be correct,' continued her tutor, 'but in a formal report or essay you must use the third person.'

'Wasn't that a famous film?' asked Susan.

'No, that was *The Third Man* and this is the first person,' stated her tutor pointing at the word 'I' in her homework.

'Why is it wrong?' asked Susan adopting a more serious attitude.

'It is wrong because it implies uncertainty when you write 'I think' or 'I feel',' answered her tutor. 'Let the evidence speak for you. It is your job to report and comment upon what you observe and to present the information in a neutral way.'

'So how should I write it?' asked Susan.

'The rise in temperature was significant because the liquid began to boil,' stated her tutor. 'It's simple, direct and avoids lots of 'I think' and 'I feel' statements which simply clutter up your writing.'

'Yes, I see what you mean,' Susan agreed.

Mohammed interprets the question

'Explain why the assassination of Archduke Franz Ferdinand led to World War One.' Mohammed stared at the essay title for his History homework and looked at his notes. 'First identify the instruction word and the key words,' thought Mohammed. He underlined the words 'Explain' and 'assassination' and 'World War One' and opened up his History file.

Mohammed found a neat list of the causes of World War One and noted that the assassination was the trigger for war rather than a major cause of war.

He listed the key reasons for the outbreak of war and identified five particular explanations. Next he turned his attention to the introduction and wrote:

> Archduke Franz Ferdinand and his wife were assassinated on 28 June 1914 while on an official tour of Sarajevo and within a month the Great Powers of Europe were preparing for war. The assassination of the heir to the Austrian throne by a Serbian terrorist organisation, the 'Black Hand', directly resulted in an Austrian decision to invade Serbia on 28 July 1914. However, the spread of the war across Europe and later the world cannot be so simply explained and there are a number of key reasons why the assassination sparked off a world war.

'Ninety-five words,' smiled Mohammed to himself, 'just within the guideline figure of 100 words maximum for an introduction.'

The guideline had forced him to be concise and to think very carefully about his choice of words otherwise he might just have rambled on as usual. It had taken five redrafts to finalise the introduction but he was happy that he had achieved a good summary of the question, picked up the key words and set a direction for his answer.

Yasmin justifies a point

'A further impact of unemployment is a feeling of being outside mainstream society and in extreme cases a sense of alienation,' read Yasmin.

Yasmin was busy writing the second paragraph of her Sociology essay on the social impact of unemployment. She was pleased with the opening sentence as it provided a direct link with the essay question. 'Next I need to expand on what I mean,' considered Yasmin. She wrote a few sentences which described what she understood by the theory of alienation and carefully checked her work against her notes on the topic. Yasmin also identified some supporting evidence for the existence of alienation from a survey and quoted the conclusions given in the textbook. 'Finally, I need a sentence to round off this paragraph and link to the next,' thought Yasmin. She wrote: 'Alienation is a significant result of unemployment as the above evidence indicates but of equal concern is the loss of the work ethic.'

In one sentence Yasmin returned to the essay theme and led the reader away from one key point and smoothly into the next.

John finds it easy

John had always found essay writing difficult because it was so hard to fill three or four sides of paper. The scale of the task always put him off and he tended to leave essays and rush them at the last minute.

John found that the essay planner sheet divided what was a major task into a series of short, easy steps. Instead of trying to focus on four sides of A4 he was fighting to reduce his words to fit the 100 word target for an introduction and he tackled the essay step-by-step. If anything his problem was editing his essays and deciding what to leave out and in doing this he was forced to think more carefully about the question and the information demanded. John's essay marks were steadily improving and he now actually enjoyed wrestling with words and writing essays.

DISCUSSION POINTS

1. Do you think that it is a fair test to write an essay in 45 minutes?

2. Should students be allowed to take textbooks into examinations?

3. Should wordprocessors be allowed into examinations? Is this the literary equivalent of whether calculators should be used for numeracy?

8
Reading for Information

At first guidance on how to read may seem unusual but reading for pleasure is very different from reading for information. When you read for pleasure you start at page one and work through to the end of the book, but when you are **reading for information** you will perhaps only read a few pages out of several books. Reading lies at the heart of A-Level study and study at university, hence the phrase 'reading for a degree'. Your tutors will recommend textbooks and most examining boards also publish reading lists. It would be foolish to ignore these books as the examiners will expect you to have referred to them. Treat the books as a store of information to dip into as and when you need to. Read for information using the **Triple S** method:

- surveying textbooks

- scanning for information

- studying the text.

SURVEYING TEXTBOOKS

Reading at A-level is rarely about reading a whole textbook but is about finding information on a particular topic to support essay writing, projects or classroom discussion. You might be lucky and find a whole textbook devoted to the relevant topic but most often it means searching several textbooks for useful references. Critically survey and select textbooks by:

- checking the **title and author** and using only recognised academic textbooks

- looking at the **last date of publication** to avoid using outdated information

- examining the **contents page** for any useful chapters on the topic

- searching the **alphabetical index** at the back of the book for any references to the topic

- examining the **bibliography** to discover other useful book titles (remember to use the Inter-Library loan service to order books not on the shelves).

This approach will save you the frustration of selecting books of minimal use. Keep surveying books until you find several textbooks with useful chapters or sections on your topic.

SCANNING FOR INFORMATION

Once you have identified useful textbooks there is no need to read every word but instead move directly to the key information using speed and scan reading techniques.

Reading at speed
A fast reading speed will allow you to scan lots of books rapidly and cut through all of the text to the exact information you need. Reading speeds do vary significantly:

- an experienced reader will read at a rate of 400 words per minute

- an average reader will read at a rate of 300 words per minute

- an inexperienced reader will read at a rate of 200 words per minute.

Discovering your own reading speed
To discover your own reading speed please read the following passage at your normal pace but time yourself in exact minutes and seconds.

LENIN'S EARLY LIFE

Lenin was born Vladimir Ilyich Ulyanov on 23 April 1870 in the small town of Simbirsk on the River Volga. The name Lenin was a pseudonym he adopted around 1900 while avoiding the secret police and he used it for the rest of his life. Lenin's mother Maria was from a wealthy German family, whereas his father Ilya Ulyanov was from a Russian peasant background.

Ilya Ulyanov excelled at school and entered teaching as a career. Maria was also a school teacher. Ilya proved to be an able administrator and was rapidly promoted to be Inspector of Schools, District Inspector and then finally Director of Public Schools for Simbirsk with the honorary status of a nobleman and the title 'Your Excellency'. Each promotion gave a higher salary and an increasingly prosperous lifestyle for the Ulyanov family. Lenin was one of six children and his childhood was relaxed and content, he was only eleven years of age in 1881 when Tsar Alexander II was assassinated. Tsar Alexander III, who succeeded to the throne, ended the reform programme initiated by Alexander II. In particular access to education was severely restricted, a measure which must have dismayed Ilya Ulyanov and provoked comment within his household. Ilya had spent his career extending the education system in Simbirsk only to watch it being withdrawn.

Ilya obviously respected education and promoted the attainment of education in his children.

In 1884 Alexander, Lenin's elder brother, gained a place at St Petersburg University. He impressed his tutors and in 1885 was awarded the University Gold Medal for outstanding academic achievement in Biology.

However, the study of Biology was not Alexander's only preoccupation. He was rapidly drawn into student politics, which was socialist and anti-Tsarist, and soon joined a revolutionary group – the People's Will. Alexander read numerous revolutionary tracts and assisted with the manufacture of explosives.

All of this activity was extremely dangerous as the secret police regarded the university as a source of dissent and employed hundreds of paid informers to spy upon the students.

On 13 January 1886 Lenin's father Ilya Ulyanov died from a brain haemorrhage. In the absence of his elder brother Lenin led the funeral procession.

Alexander, at university, was now actively planning with other students to assassinate the Tsar. The students made bombs and planned to assassinate the Tsar as he processed along Nevsky Prospekt, St Petersburg's main street.

Alexander and the student revolutionaries waited several times for the Tsar to appear without success. On 1 March 1887 Alexander and the other students were all arrested by the secret police as they waited on Nevsky Prospekt. Police informers had penetrated the revolutionary cell months before and had monitored each stage of the assassination plot.

Lenin's mother was deeply shocked by Alexander's involvement in the assassination plot. On 25 April 1887, despite his mother's appeals for clemency, Alexander was sentenced to death along with 14 other students. On 8 May 1887 the sentence was carried out and he was executed by a firing squad.

There is no record of the impact of these events upon Lenin but, given his later actions, this was clearly a watershed.

Lenin was now aged 17 and anxious to proceed to university to study Law. However, his application was immediately refused as his brother had been executed for terrorism. The headteacher of Lenin's school, F M Kerensky, strongly supported Lenin's application and his reference reminded the authorities of Ilya Ulyanov's service and firmly recommended Lenin for a university place.

Lenin was admitted to Kazan University in August 1887. Hidden among his Law books were most of Alexander's books which Lenin had retrieved. He was desperately trying to understand what had influenced and motivated his brother.

The name of Alexander Ulyanov was well known to the students as a revolutionary hero and Lenin was the proud recipient of student pride and expectation. Lenin did not disappoint his fellow students and was soon deeply involved in student politics, taking part in anti-Tsarist protests in the university on 4 December 1887. On 5 December 1887 Lenin resigned his place at university and was formally expelled and, in common with many anti-Tsarists activists, exiled.

Lenin later joined the Social Democratic Party and argued fiercely for the Party to plan revolution against the Tsar. The Party divided over the issue and Lenin rapidly took charge of the revolutionary wing, the Bolsheviks.

On the night of 6/7 November 1917 the Bolsheviks seized control of the capital city St Petersburg in the world's first successful communist revolution.

Calculating your reading speed
How did you do? Check your reading speed against the following scale.

Time taken	Words per minute (reading speed)
5m	148
4m 30	164
4m	184
3m 30	211
3m	246
2m 30	296
2m 15	328
2m	370
1m 45	422

If you reading speed is below 300 words a minute then this is much too slow for scan reading and you will need to improve. An inexperienced reader tends to read every word or even worse mouth each word while reading. Both habits will place your reading speed into a straitjacket!

Scan reading

The scan reading technique is to read **groups of words** at a time and to mentally sift sentences for the key words which convey the meaning of the sentence. Look at this example:

$$1 \qquad 2 \qquad 3 \qquad 4 \quad 5 \quad 6 \qquad 7$$
The torch beam pierced the darkness and lit up the doorway.

The inexperienced reader will take approximately seven eye movements to read the above sentence, as indicated. The key words which convey the meaning in this sentence are simply *torch beam, darkness* and *doorway*. The experienced reader will mentally sift sentences for the key words and ignore the rest. To scan read imagine that each page of a textbook has a vertical line running down the centre of the page. Fix your eyes on this invisible line and move your eye down the page flicking across each line of text from left to right scanning for key words. Don't underestimate the speed at which the brain works. Your memory will instantly recognise and absorb common words like the, and, it, up etc. These are joining words, the basic cement of any sentence. Train yourself to sift sentences for the key words and your reading speed will soon increase.

The purpose of scan reading is to locate only the information you need and to ignore the rest. Keep the name or theory you are researching in your mind while you scan read and it will trigger you to stop once you hit the relevant words.

STUDYING THE TEXT

Once you have identified a useful passage it is necessary to extract information and here you need to switch from scan reading to study reading.

Slowly read each sentence, one word at a time, taking notes as you proceed. If the book belongs to you then use a highlighter pen and make notes in the margin to remind you of key points. Your reading speed may drop to as low as 50 words a minute but this reflects the need for careful reading and absorbing what may be unfamiliar concepts. Take your time to:

- use a dictionary to define difficult words or terms

- list questions for yourself and ask your tutor to explain

- record useful quotations

- identify the explanation of a particular theory/concept.

Remember to record the book title, author and page number on every sheet of notes so that you can return directly to the information source. This will be important if you intend to use quotations as the source must always be quoted.

Buying books
In general try to get into a book-buying habit. Books are the tools of your trade and regular reading will take you above and beyond the set text and into a much deeper understanding and appreciation of your study topics. Take a pride in building up a book collection and visit a good bookshop whenever you are in town and note the wealth of information that exists on any topic. Tutors prepare their lessons from textbooks so why not cut out the middle man or woman and read ahead the **Triple S** way:

SURVEY

SCAN

STUDY.

CHECKLIST

Develop your reading skills by:

- surveying and discriminating on your choice of textbooks

- increasing your reading speed

- scanning text for useful information

- using study reading to extract information

- highlighting key points in the text

- extracting useful quotations and evidence

- applying the **Triple S** method.

CASE STUDIES

Susan surveys textbooks

Susan glanced along the book titles on the library shelf. There were lots of Chemistry textbooks but nothing directly on the subject of gases.

'Right!' she muttered to herself, 'let's conduct a survey and find something useful.'

After ten minutes spent flicking through textbooks Susan identified three textbooks with whole chapters on gases and a further two textbooks with sections on gases which she had located from the book indexes. All five books were recent editions written by experienced lecturers in chemistry.

'Perfect,' thought Susan as she headed for the library desk.

Mohammed increases his reading speed

Mohammed paused in his reading. He was doing it! He was mouthing each word under his breath as he read. 'No wonder my reading speed is low,' thought Mohammed.

He turned over to the next page in the textbook and placed his finger in the centre of the first line of text. He scanned the line from left to right and dropped his finger down to the next line.

'Bismarck, Bismarck!' he kept thinking to himself as he scanned.

'Bismarck!' screamed Mohammed's brain as he tripped across the name halfway down the page and stopped scanning. Mohammed reached for his notepad, having located a useful passage on Bismarck, the founder of the Second German Reich in 1871.

Yasmin studies the text

Yasmin sat hunched over a Psychology textbook at a library table. She had found two chapters directly on the subject of crime and deviance and was busy digesting them word by word. She kept a Psychology subject dictionary by her elbow to look up the words she did not understand and was making slow but certain progress. Yasmin placed the book title and author at the top of a page of notes and wrote a summary of the author's views on crime and deviance. She took care to put it in her own words so that she did not repeat whole sentences and find herself guilty of plagiarism, but did record one or two useful quotations to use as evidence in essays.

John questions the booklist

John looked at the booklist for Economics and thought to himself, 'you must be joking.'

There were at least 50 book titles on it! 'No one can read all of these?' questioned John.

'I agree,' said his tutor. 'You are not expected to read every word of every book. Some of the books are particularly good for one topic and others for other topics.'

'So what do we read?' asked John.

'You select chapters and sections as you need them,' replied his tutor. 'Try to follow the order of study and dip into the booklist and find good supporting information as we go along.'

John nodded in agreement and was glad he had questioned the booklist otherwise he would just have ignored it as impossible.

DISCUSSION POINTS

1. Given the necessary books do you actually need a tutor?

2. Why is it important to be able to locate information for yourself?

3. Why are textbooks more difficult to read than general fiction? Can you identify what makes the difference? How can you overcome this?

9
Researching Coursework

Most A-Level subjects now involve coursework, which means assembling a jigsaw of information from many separate sources. A significant proportion of your coursework marks will be devoted to your ability to **research information**. The higher you progress academically the more you will be expected to undertake research until finally at PhD level you will be expected to conduct research which yields original information. In some A-Level subjects primary research will be expected – *ie* field visits, surveys, questionnaires – but in most cases research means using library sources. Once your coursework title has been approved by your tutor and the examining board you must consider carefully all of the possible sources of information.

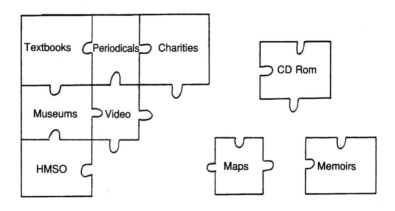

FINDING INFORMATION

Where possible try to use sources of information beyond textbooks to demonstrate that you are aware of other sources. You might consider:

Atlases
Audio tapes
Banks
Biographies
CD Roms
Charities
Dictionary of quotations
Company records
Consumer councils
Church archives
Computer databases
Central Statistical Office publications
Citizens Advice Bureau
Documents
Directories of business/industry
Encyclopaedias
Gazetteer
Government departments
HMSO publications
Humanities index
Keesings Archives
Letters
Local authority records
Magazines
Maps
Memoirs
Memoirs
Museums
Music
Paintings
Periodicals
Photographs
Professional organisations
Public relations officers
Newspapers
Radio
Television
Trade unions
Video
Year books

Many of these immediate sources of information will be in your school/college library but if not try a major public library, *ie* a city library rather than a small branch library. If you live near a university ask if you can use the library facilities. You will not be able to borrow books but you may gain permission to study in the library.

USING THE LIBRARY

Modern libraries contain much more than textbooks and you must systematically consult and exhaust all sources of information:

- textbooks
- reference books
- periodicals
- video
- CD Rom.

Searching for textbooks

Looking directly at the books on the library shelf is not the best way to find textbooks as at any one time many books will be out on loan. Also consider if you were a librarian where would you place, for example, *The History of the Motor Car*?

- In the History section?
- In the Transport section?
- In the Technology section?

The only certain way to find all of the textbooks on a particular topic is to use the library catalogue. Some library catalogues will be on computer but most will still be a card index system normally sited near the library entrance. A library catalogue will have two sections:

Using the author catalogue
This is a straight A to Z index by author surname. If you have a book-list use the author catalogue to see if the books are held by the library. Remember that a library will reserve a book for you if it is out on loan. A library can also order any book you need on Inter Library loan.

Using the subject catalogue
This is an index of subject headings and it is often a good place to start topic research. Find your topic and the index card will list all of the relevant textbooks held by the library. You may have to be creative in looking up your topic, *eg* nothing under 'Urban problems'? Try 'Inner city'?

Both catalogues will give you **classification** numbers. The author catalogue will provide a unique number for the individual book concerned and the subject catalogue a unique number for the subject area. If you look carefully you will see that these numbers are printed on the ends of book shelves, on the individual shelves and finally on the spine of each book in the library. Follow the classification numbers to locate first the section and then the particular book you want to consult.

Most libraries use the Dewey Decimal System invented by an American librarian, Melvin Dewey, in 1876. The Dewey system classifies all books into ten sections:

000 – 099	General Knowledge books (ie most reference books)
100 – 199	Philosophy
200 – 299	Religions
300 – 399	Sociology and Economics
400 – 499	Languages
500 – 599	Natural Sciences
600 – 699	Applied Science
700 – 799	Arts, Crafts, Sports

800 – 899   Literature (Fiction is normally separate)
900 – 999   History, Geography.

The Dewey Decimal System has stood the test of time and the categories are sufficiently broad to absorb subjects like Computing, Genetics, Flight and Nuclear Power – all unknown to Dewey. Which category do you think they are all under? Easy, isn't it?

All of the number sequences given above cover a host of related sub-sections and eventually allow a unique number to be generated for an individual book. Once you know the Dewey classification numbers for your topic and A-Level subjects you will be able to rapidly locate books in any library operating the Dewey system.

Finally, when you have found useful textbooks always check at the back of the book for a bibliography for further useful book titles. Check the author catalogue to see if the library stocks the other books and if not order them on the Inter Library Loan Service. Enquire at the library counter.

Looking in reference books

The reference section of a library can provide lots of up-to-date and summary information and give you an immediate overview of a topic which may help you to plan and shape your research. A good reference section will offer a selection of sources as follows:

Indexes
There are millions of articles published in magazines, newspapers and periodicals every year, but how do you know if something was published on your topic?

The answer is to look in an Index which will list topic by topic all of the articles published. You can then order a photocopy of the relevant article. The major index is the *British Humanities Index* but others also exist. Ask your librarian.

Dictionaries
Apart from major English dictionaries expect to find foreign language dictionaries, subject dictionaries for all of your A-Level subjects and dictionaries of quotations and literature.

Encyclopaedias
Britannica is excellent for an immediate overview of any topic but also look for other specialist encyclopaedias, the *Oxford Companion* series which gives an individual volume to most subjects, the

Guinness guides, *Larousse Encyclopaedia of Music, etc.*

Year books
A variety of year books provide up-to-date information in the rapidly changing fields of politics, education, defence, industry, *etc.* Look for *Whitakers Almanac, Fact Finder, Pears Cyclopaedia, Statesman's Year Book, Info '95 etc.*

Recent events
Where was that earthquake six months ago? *Keesings Record of World Events* is a complete summary month by month of all significant events across the world. Annual volumes are collated.

Atlases
Many specialist subject atlases are published *eg* Biblical, Historical, Economic.

Government
The government – meaning all departments, commissions, committees and enquiries – publishes lots of reports every year with often the most up-to-date findings and research on any topic. Look in the *HMSO Annual Catalogue* for a complete listing of every publication and order anything useful.

Statistics
The Central Statistical Office collates and presents national statistics on most aspects of government and society. Look back to Chapter 6 for a listing of the individual sources.

General
Who's Who and *Who Was Who* for instant references to prominent people. A gazetteer for an up-to-date overview of a foreign country. *The Art Book* or a history of art for an overview of art *etc.*

Finally, if you want to know how to address a duke or an archbishop look in *Debrett's Correct Form* and you won't embarrass yourself!

Periodicals
This is the proper term for an academic weekly or periodic publication as opposed to a general interest magazine. Look in W H Smith and see the enormous range of periodicals and magazines and even they don't

stock everything! A library will stock a range of periodicals along with the daily newspapers. These are often good sources of relevant up-to-date articles and the library will stock all of the back copies. To save time flicking through a large stack of periodicals hoping to find a relevant article use the *British Humanities Index* or a more specialist index as described above under reference books.

Video

Most libraries will contain a video section and a playback facility to view the tapes. Check for video tapes relevant to your topic and perhaps discover acknowledged subject experts discussing and presenting information on your topic. Look for any accompanying notes and associated booklists.

CD Rom

CD represents the modern face of the library and perhaps the future for most reference books and other printed matter. Already you can interrogate CD encyclopaedias which combine text, video and still pictures – some are even interactive, allowing you to pose questions. A whole year's newspaper like the *Guardian* or *The Times* can now be placed on a single CD and you can rapidly locate any articles published on any topic just by entering key words. This field is expanding rapidly so check what is available. *The Times* is now also available on the Internet. So if you have a computer at home why wait for the newspaper to be delivered, just come down to breakfast and print out your own copy.

Allow several weeks for your research to give sufficient time to:

- examine all possible sources

- write letters to relevant organisations

- visit relevant museums or exhibitions

- receive books on Inter Library Loan.

WRITING YOUR STUDY

When you are ready to write the first draft of your personal study follow the advice on essay writing in Chapter 7. It is simply a question of scale but maintain the same approach and the same sections. Your key points may become chapters but as with essay key points ensure that each chapter is interlinked and contributes to the overall conclusion. If you subdivide your study in this way you will soon reach the word total – if anything the problem will be how to edit and reduce your points.

Seek your tutor's guidance for your chapter headings and present a first draft for comment before completing your final personal study.

PRESENTING YOUR STUDY

Apply basic psychology and impress the examiner with a neat professional presentation. This means:

- buying a flat, plastic binder with a clear cover

- printing a clear title page and inserting it into the cover

- providing a contents page

- writing an introduction

- dividing into chapters or at least a succession of individual points

- using relevant evidence but keeping quotations brief

- referring to and discussing any quotations or evidence

- ending with a conclusion which answers your enquiry

- listing all books and sources of information.

It is not necessary to wordprocess your personal study but where possible please do. Wordprocessing is a more impressive presentation and it is fast becoming a university requirement. It is also a painless way of altering your draft when your tutor says, 'I think you ought to include . . .'.

Finally, regardless of how well you present your study it must be based upon good research, so make the effort to research widely and earn the marks.

CHECKLIST

Research coursework topics by:

- considering the full range of information sources

- writing to relevant organisations

- visiting relevant museums and exhibitions

- using the library catalogue to pinpoint relevant textbooks

- requesting books on Inter Library Loan
- searching the reference section
- checking back copies of periodicals and newspapers
- viewing relevant video tapes
- interrogating CD Roms
- taking notes from all sources
- consulting your tutor.

CASE STUDIES

Susan locates soda water

Susan flicked through a further Chemistry book but she could not find the general background information on oxygen that she wanted for her introduction.

'Encyclopaedias,' muttered Susan to herself, 'of course!'

The index gave a variety of references to oxygen and Susan turned to Discovery. 'Joseph Priestley discovers oxygen in 1774,' she read, and began to make some notes. After 15 minutes Susan had gathered more than enough information but she also decided to check the Biography section of the library to see if a biography of Priestley existed. It might be interesting for a general read. She was about to close the encyclopaedia when the words 'soda water' caught her eye. 'Priestley invented soda water in 1772,' read Susan. 'Now that will make an excellent footnote!'

Mohammed reserves a book

Mohammed didn't know where to look for a copy of Desmond Morris's book, *Manwatching*.

'It could be Biology I suppose?' thought Mohammed as he wandered out of the Psychology section. He noticed the sign 'Author Catalogue'.

'Worth a try, I suppose.'

In a matter of seconds Mohammed found an index card for Desmond Morris and discovered that Morris had also written *The Naked Ape*. He jotted down the Dewey numbers given on the index cards and followed the number system to the right shelf. *Manwatching* was there but *The Naked Ape* was not. Mohammed took *Manwatching* to the library counter and reserved *The Naked Ape*.

'It will be held for you at the counter as soon as it is returned,' confirmed the librarian.

'All too easy,' smiled Mohammed to himself.

Yasmin discovers hundreds of articles

'I've never heard of half of these periodicals before,' thought Yasmin as she scanned through all of the references to the topic of Family in the *British Humanities Index*. 'I'll have to be selective, and choose what seems the most useful.' She sat down at a table and slowly read the title and description of each article on the family published in Britain in 1994.

After 15 minutes Yasmin went to the library counter, asked to see the relevant back copies of three periodicals held by the library and ordered four photocopies of articles from periodicals not held by the library.

'Find anything?' asked Yasmin's tutor at the next lesson.

'Too much,' laughed Yasmin, 'there were hundreds of articles in the 1994 volume alone.'

John is interactive

'Is this the whole of the *Encyclopaedia Britannica*?' asked John.

'It is,' replied the librarian as he slotted a single CD Rom into the library computer.

'All 44 millions words and 2,500 illustration are in here,' confirmed the librarian as he accessed the main menu.

'So how do I . . .?'

'Just ask it a question, it is interactive,' laughed the librarian.

'What is the Gold Standard?' typed John and within seconds he was presented with the answer and given references for more detailed reading.

The librarian left John as he browsed through other topics from his A-Level Economics. It was so easy to search and find information and then print out copies of anything useful.

DISCUSSION POINTS

1.   Will there still be a place for books in 20 years' time?

2.   Is an ability to research important?

3.   How big a percentage of the overall marks for an A-Level do you think should be allocated to coursework?

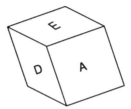

Do not leave your final 'A'-Level grade to a celestial roll of the die but instead review your progress regularly and seek ways to improve.

ASSESSING YOUR POTENTIAL

First, gain a realistic assessment of your potential A-Level grades by examining your GCSE grades. Research conducted by the Audit Commission and HMI has established a correlation between GCSE grades and future A-Level results.

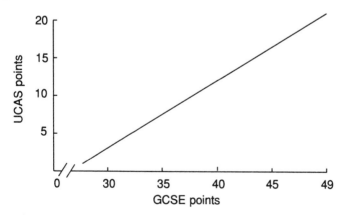

Fig. 22. GCSE and A-Level correlation.

113

The graph in Figure 22 gives GCSE grades as numerical scores along the horizontal axis and the university entrance (UCAS) scores for A-Level on the vertical axis.

Predict your A-Level performance

Convert your GCSE grades to a numerical score using the formula given in Appendix B and predict your own A-Level performance. The formula works best for low and medium GCSE scores. A high score will basically indicate a Grade A potential but not pinpoint the exact number of Grade As.

Next, do not assume that the die has been cast! This is your minimum potential. It is your starting position. A promising student may end up with low A-Level grades and vice versa. The answer is to monitor your own progress and aim to exceed your potential.

Using ALIS

The School of Education at Newcastle upon Tyne University has extended the GCSE A-Level correlation in the ALIS project (A-Level Information System) which, for a fee, provides participating schools and colleges with a full analysis of predicted and actual results. Approximately 170 schools and colleges currently use the ALIS service to measure the effectiveness of their A-Level courses, so you may find yourself completing ALIS questionnaires.

MAKING SENSE OF ASSESSMENTS

Few schools or colleges have a set marking standard or marking criteria which all staff adhere to, and marking schemes will also vary between staff. Some will use percentage marks, some grades and some will mark out of 20 or 25. To help you make sense of these different marks here is the approximate A-Level marks standard:

Grade	Percentage mark
A	70 +
B	60 – 69
C	53 – 59
D	46 – 52
E	40 – 45
N	33 – 39 Narrow Fail
U	0 – 32 Unclassified Fail

If you are given marks out of 20 or 25 then simply multiply by 5 or 4 respectively to convert to a percentage and read off above.

These grade boundaries are approximate, so do not regard the above as the absolute standard but rather as a guide to the standard. Checking your progress is important but try not to become fixed on marks and remember that you have two years to reach the standard. A good tutor will demand more of you term by term rather than marking to a strict A-Level standard from your first day. Finally, be realistic about your standard of work and especially for UCAS applications. Consider your A-Level potential and the marks band where most of your homework falls when deciding which universities to apply to. Try not to have a false impression of your ability or you may be disappointed once the results are published.

Recording your progress

Record your marks and, importantly, your tutor's comments and advice by ruling a table as shown in Figure 23.

Subject:		Tutor:	
Homework	Weaknesses	Ways to improve

Fig. 23. Recording your progress.

Too many students who receive low marks simply ram the offending homework into their bags to be forgotten. If your mark was 40 per cent, why was it not 70 per cent? What was missing?

Ask your tutors. Trust their judgement and work with them. Seek ways to improve and act on their advice. Learn from marks – do not ignore them!

QUESTIONING YOURSELF

If your marks remain low first question yourself and your commitment to study. Test your commitment by completing the following questionnaire. Please tick your immediate, truthful response to each question.

Study questionnaire

Questions	Often	Sometimes	Never
1. I attend all lessons	____	____	____
2. I take lots of notes	____	____	____
3. I read ahead	____	____	____
4. I give my best to every homework	____	____	____
5. I ask when I don't understand	____	____	____
6. I regularly study in the library	____	____	____
7. I buy books and study aids	____	____	____
8. I watch relevant TV programmes	____	____	____
9. I correct my English	____	____	____
10. I question my progress	____	____	____
11. I use a studytime planner	____	____	____
12. I fully revise for all assessments	____	____	____

Score: 3 marks for each Often tick.
          2 marks for each Sometimes tick.
          1 mark for each Never tick.

Add up your marks and read off your score below:

27 – 36 marks. **Excellent.** You possess high motivation and are very much in charge of your studies and should gain a Grade A.

19 – 26 marks **Good.** You work hard and only need to slightly upgrade your study performance towards assessments to gain a high grade.

13 – 18 marks **Satisfactory.** You are not taking an organised approach to your studies and need to take more positive action to improve.

0 – 12 marks **Below standard.** Are you sure you are an A-Level student? Re-read this study guide and put all of the advice given into action.

If you are fulfilling your side of the bargain and working to full capacity then you probably need more time and help to adjust to A-Level standard. There is a considerable leap from GCSE to A-Level and you must be certain what is expected of you. Seek your tutor's support and take advantage of the many study aids on the market.

USING STUDY AIDS

Sometimes no matter what you do your progress remains slow because:

- you find the textbook difficult

- your tutor goes too fast

- you just can't understand a topic

- your essays are weak.

Instead of deciding you are no good at a particular subject boost your performance by buying some **study aids** from a good bookshop or by mail order. The following study aids are all useful purchases and may help you to improve.

For subject support
- *Macmillan Mastering Series*. Cover most A-Level subjects and give an easy to read overview of the entire subject. Read alongside your textbook.

- *Penguin subject dictionaries*. Excellent for instant references to key words, names, terms, theories.

- *Philip Allan A-Level Review*. Covers most subjects in a bright, informative magazine published four times per year. Lots of pictures, diagrams, statistics, tables, examiners' comments and up-to-date articles on key topics.

- *Fast Forward A-Level Tapes*. Lectures on key topics you can listen to on your personal stereo over and over again with accompanying study packs.

- *Enterprise Education*. Conferences covering key topics led by A-Level examiners and authors of leading textbooks.

For essay writing support
- *How to Write an Essay*, How To Books Ltd.

- *Richard Ball Publishing*. Volumes of sample essays and How To Write Good Essays.

For revision support
Consider buying an A-Level subject guide which will summarise all of the key points and give useful exam information:

- *Letts A-Level Study Guides*

- *Longman A-Level Revise Guides*

- *Longman York Guides for Literature*

- *Macmillan Work Out Series.*

For sets of revision notes:

- *Richard Ball Publishing.*

For study skills support
- *How To Books Ltd*. A variety of useful books in this series on different aspects of study skills, *eg* writing assignments, using the library.

- *Macmillan Mastering Series: study skills.*

For exam support

- *How to Pass Exams Without Anxiety*, How To Books Ltd.

- *Fast Forward*. Exam Success audio tape for advice on revision techniques and stress reduction produced by the famous hypnotist Paul McKenna and Michael Breen.

Some of the above study aids are mail order only (see Useful Addresses). This list is not exhaustive and you should check your library shelves and bookshops carefully for other useful study aids.

CHECKLIST

Improve your progress by:

- calculating your GCSE score and discovering your A-Level potential

- monitoring your marks against the A-Level standard

- recording ways to improve

- questioning your commitment to study

- buying useful study aids

- seeking support from your tutor.

CASE STUDIES

Susan calculates her potential
Susan had passed ten GCSEs, all with A and B grades. She studied the numerical scoring system as given in Appendix A and discovered that she had a points total of 46.

'Doesn't sound very high,' thought Susan.

She looked at the graph and was delighted to see that 46 points was 18.8 points on the UCAS scale taking her into the Grade A zone.

'It's good,' she thought. 'Oxford or Cambridge will demand 30 points or three A-levels at Grade A so it's reassuring to know that I should reach Grade A standard.'

Mohammed checks his marks
'Do not,' emphasised Mohammed's tutor as he returned some homework, 'measure your marks too harshly against the A-Level marks standard. Remember that you have two full years to reach the standard but do monitor your standard and gain a general impression of your ability.'

Mohammed looked at his essay and saw 56 per cent circled at the top of the first page. He felt disappointed but on turning to the A-Level marks bands he noted that although 56 per cent represented a Grade C he was only four marks away from the Grade B marks band. 'That's my target,' thought Mohammed. 'I can easily improve my performance by at least four per cent and gain a Grade B.' He looked back at his essay and began to read the tutor's comments for suggestions on ways to improve.

Yasmin finds a way to improve
'I just can't understand Durkheim,' complained Yasmin to her tutor.

'What's the problem?' enquired her tutor.

'Listen to this sentence,' said Yasmin and she quoted aloud: '"When he neglects the distinction between the conclusion or inference which ends the search for an explanation and the empirical demonstration of a relationship between particular variables." It's so confusing.'

'Yes, the level of language is difficult, but it is necessary to ensure precision in communicating the ideas and theories,' sympathised her tutor. 'Wait a moment,' and she pulled out a copy of *Mastering Sociology*, published by Macmillan Press.

'Read the relevant chapter in here,' said her tutor. 'It's written in very straightforward clear English and then go back to the textbook.'

The following lesson Yasmin returned the book.

'Well?' asked her tutor.

'Durkheim's easy,' laughed Yasmin, 'and thanks – I've brought my own copy to use with future topics.'

John decides to work harder

John studied his low assessment marks with concern. He thought he was improving but his marks were not moving out of the 40–45 per cent marks band or basically a Grade E. He put a brave face on it with his mates but he was unhappy. John turned to the short questionnaire on commitment to study and answered the questions. His performance was rated 14 or just into the Satisfactory band. John looked closely at his answers and realised that although he was attending all classes and taking loads of notes he was doing very little else. He spent his time between lessons sitting chatting and his evenings going out or watching TV. He hadn't really appreciated before the tasks expected of him as a student and he had dropped into bad habits without even realising it. John got out some paper and ruled a studytime planner for the week ahead. It was time to get some studying done!

DISCUSSION POINTS

1. Do you think that the A-Level grade boundaries are fair?

2. Do you think that you work hard enough? What is your study routine for a typical week?

3. What study aids have you found useful and would recommend to others?

11
Preparing for Examinations

Do not be frightened by the prospect of examinations. Welcome them! This is your moment after two years of hard work and with good revision you will actually enjoy the experience of answering the questions. Take comfort from the recently published book *Actualising Talent* by Professor Michael Howe of Exeter University, a psychologist who specialises in the study of high achievers. His research indicates that genius owes more to hard and sustained work rather than to high intelligence. All you have to do is meet the challenge!

MEETING THE CHALLENGE

First, discover exactly what your A-Level examinations involve:

- How many separate examination papers per subject?
- Is each examination paper divided into sections?
- How many questions must be answered per section?
- What topic areas does each paper and section examine?
- Which topics are regularly examined?
- What topics are only occasionally examined?
- What do the examiners expect?

You can answer all of these questions by reference to:

- the examination board syllabus book (select the year of your exam)
- past examination papers
- examiners' reports
- scheme of work
- your tutor.

Your school or college library should keep all of this information in the reference section, but if you have difficulty write to the publications department of the relevant examinations board (see Useful Addresses) and request an order form. Look back over a minimum of three and preferably five years' past examinations papers and examiners' reports to absorb the pattern of questions and the examiners' advice and recommendations. Capture all of this information as shown in Figure 24. Use the syllabus, scheme of work and past papers to complete the following table:

Examination format					
Subject:			**Board:**		
Exam paper	Paper section	Question type	Topic areas	Time limit	No. of answers

Fig. 24. Identifying exam requirements.

Use the past examination papers, the syllabus and your tutor's guidance to complete the table in Figure 25.

Revision Topics Indicator						
Subject:					**Paper:**	
Year	Topic 1	Topic 2	Topic 3	Topic 4	Topic 5 etc.	Examiners' comments

Fig. 25. Listing key revision topics.

The purpose of the table is to highlight whether syllabus topics are examined regularly or only occasionally and to make you familiar with the question styles. Enter all of the key topic titles across the top of the table in the spaces marked 'topic'. Rule as many columns as you have topics and if need be stick several sheets of paper together. Take your earliest past paper and enter the year into the left hand column and then enter each examination question under the appropriate topic heading. When you have entered a minimum of three past exam papers you will see at a glance the topic areas examined every year and the frequency of the rest. Use this table to identify the core topic areas for revision but only after discussion with your tutor. The more years you can enter the more reliable the topic indicator will be.

Counting the topics

Decide with your tutor the **key topics areas** which should be revised. If you have to answer four questions in a three-hour examination how many topics should you revise? Obviously not just four! You must have a safety margin in case a regular topic does not appear or the wording of the question does not suit you. So how many revision topics? A minimum of six topics and a maximum of eight will place you in a commanding position. Ensure that your tutor approves your final list of revision topics.

Counting the weeks

It is a common mistake to start revision too late and then to drop revision topics as the weeks run out. Do not be fooled into thinking that the second year of A-Level is actually a year! The first examinations will arrive in the last week of May with the main exam period starting in June. The academic year will vary in different areas but the maximum time period September to June is:

40 WEEKS

This figure includes all holidays and is the **total number of weeks available**. If you estimate a minimum of ten revision topics per A-Level this means:

- 30 topics to be known to exam standard for three A-Levels!
- 40 topics if you are taking four A-Levels.

This is a topic a week if you start revising from September, but the first term is normally taken up with completing coursework and you might wish to deduct holidays as follows:

- 15 weeks for the first term

- 2 weeks for Christmas holidays
- 1 week for February half term
- 2 weeks for Easter holidays

which reduces the time for revision down to:

20 WEEKS

Once you divide a minimum of 30 topics into 20 weeks you are down to counting the number of days to be allocated to the revision of each topic!

This revision arithmetic will vary for each person according to the number of A-Level subjects and the topics for revision. Check the arithmetic for your own revision programme and do not let the weeks slip away.

REVISING TOPICS

Do not be intimidated by the arithmetic but rather let it spur you into action to implement your revision programme. Twenty weeks *is* sufficient time for revision as the millions who have gone before can testify. Immediately after Christmas put your revision plan into action by:

- preparing a weekly revision planner
- collating topic notes
- condensing notes
- creating key cards.

Preparing a revision planner

Look back to the directions for creating a studytime planner given in Chapter 2 and use the same approach to direct your revision. Between Christmas and Easter aim to work for four nights out of seven and after Easter take this up to five nights allowing two nights off for rest and relaxation. The cinema and discos will still be open after July so keep to this schedule and earn your nights off! It is advisable to mix your subject revision topics rather than revising all of your History and then all of your Sociology *etc*. Each evening of your planner should look like Figure 26.

Revision planner				
Day	6 – 7	7 – 8	8 – 9	9 – 10

Fig. 26. Weekly revision planner.

Prepare a revision planner for a week ahead and block out your three or two evenings off according to different social commitments. Aim to complete three one-hour revision sessions per revision evening. Take one of the above hours off to rest or to watch a favourite programme. Try and use your rest hour to break up the evening so that you are not working for longer than two hours at a time.

The planner stops at 10pm but if you are more of a night owl then adjust the times to suit – but do complete three hours' revision each evening.

Keep to this schedule for four and later five nights out of seven and you will soon make rapid progress and also keep up with your social life. Use your daytime hours and the weekends to keep up with homework and other study demands.

Collating topic notes

This is your first revision stage and if you have followed the advice given in Chapter 3 then most of the necessary information will be sitting in your subject files. First create a **revision file** for each of your A-Level subjects and make the first page of each file a revision checklist as shown in Figure 27.

Revision checklist				
Revision topics	Collated	Condensed	Key card	Status

Fig. 27. Revision checklist.

This is your at-a-glance revision checklist so that as the weeks pass you have a record of what you have done and what remains to be done. List all the key topics for revision down the left hand column and as you complete the revision stages described below place a tick in the relevant box. The final Status column is to record in your final revision weeks how well you know and can remember the information listed on your key cards. This is the information you will carry in your memory into the exam room. Simply write in 'done' or if you wish devise a colour code system for how well you know a topic or to show where more revision is required.

Stage One of your revision process is to collate all of your class notes, handouts and notes from the course textbook and library textbooks. Check that nothing is missing and staple together. Read through all of the notes and check your understanding. Does it all make sense? If not consult your tutor. When you are happy with your notes and your understanding place a tick in the Collated box of your revision checklist.

Condensing your notes

Once you have placed a tick for 'collated' against all of your revision topics you are ready to move forward to Stage Two and to condense your notes. Rewrite all of your notes into a **brief summary** of the key points and key evidence. Look at the past exam questions on each topic and if you have bought subject revision guides incorporate any useful information. Aim to condense everything to lists: names, dates, theories, opinions, explanations – whatever is appropriate. Bring your lists to life using **revision wheels**, as in Figure 28.

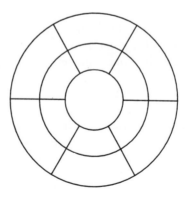

Fig. 28. Drawing a revision wheel.

Place your topic title in the wheel hub and if there are six key points draw six spokes as indicated above. Use the inner circle for the key points and the outer circle for related, supporting information. This is good visual stimulation and it will help you to absorb and to make sense of your notes.

Creating key cards

Here you are going to record all of the essential information for one topic on a single card. It is a good idea to use card rather than paper as it is durable and easy to handle. You can buy small record cards from any stationery shop or use blank postcards. The layout is as shown in Figure 29.

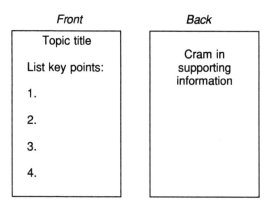

Fig. 29. Creating key cards.

If the back of the card does not allow you sufficient space to elaborate then lift each key point onto a separate card and staple all of your cards together into one topic set.

Learning and remembering

By the time you have completed the key card stage for all of your topics you will surprise yourself with how much you know and can remember. Your task is to learn and remember the information on your key cards. The rest of the information is already lodged in your mind and by simply listing and remembering the key points you will trigger it. In your final revision weeks it is time to pace the room repeating the information on your key cards:

- read the key points five times

- take a blank page and write the points from memory

- check your memory against the card

- repeat until you are perfect

- draw a revision wheel from memory.

This is tiring work so break off every 20 minutes:

- pace the room

- make a coffee

- listen to some music

- tidy your wardrobe

but then back to it!

Writing skeleton essays

If your examinations involve essay writing them remember that examinations only allow 45 minutes per essay. Look back to Chapter 7 and the detailed guidance on essay writing and as a part of your revision programme practise writing essays to time. This will test your knowledge of key topics and improve your ability to write essays under exam conditions. To cover lots of topics in a short space of time copy the planner sheet in Figure 30 and write skeleton essays as follows:

- **Planning**: study the question and plan your answer. Identify key points. *5 mins.*

- **Introduction**: Write an introduction of no more than 100 words. *5 mins.*

- **Main text**: List the key points you think will provide a good answer but do not write in full – simply list the points.

- **Conclusion**: Summarise your argument in 200 words maximum. *10 mins.*

Write skeleton essays on all of the past exam questions you can find and ask your tutor for essay titles. Practise and practise until you can comfortably meet the timings given. These times will leave you with 25 minutes in the exam to write your main text in full rather than just listing the points, keeping you within a total of 45 minutes per essay.

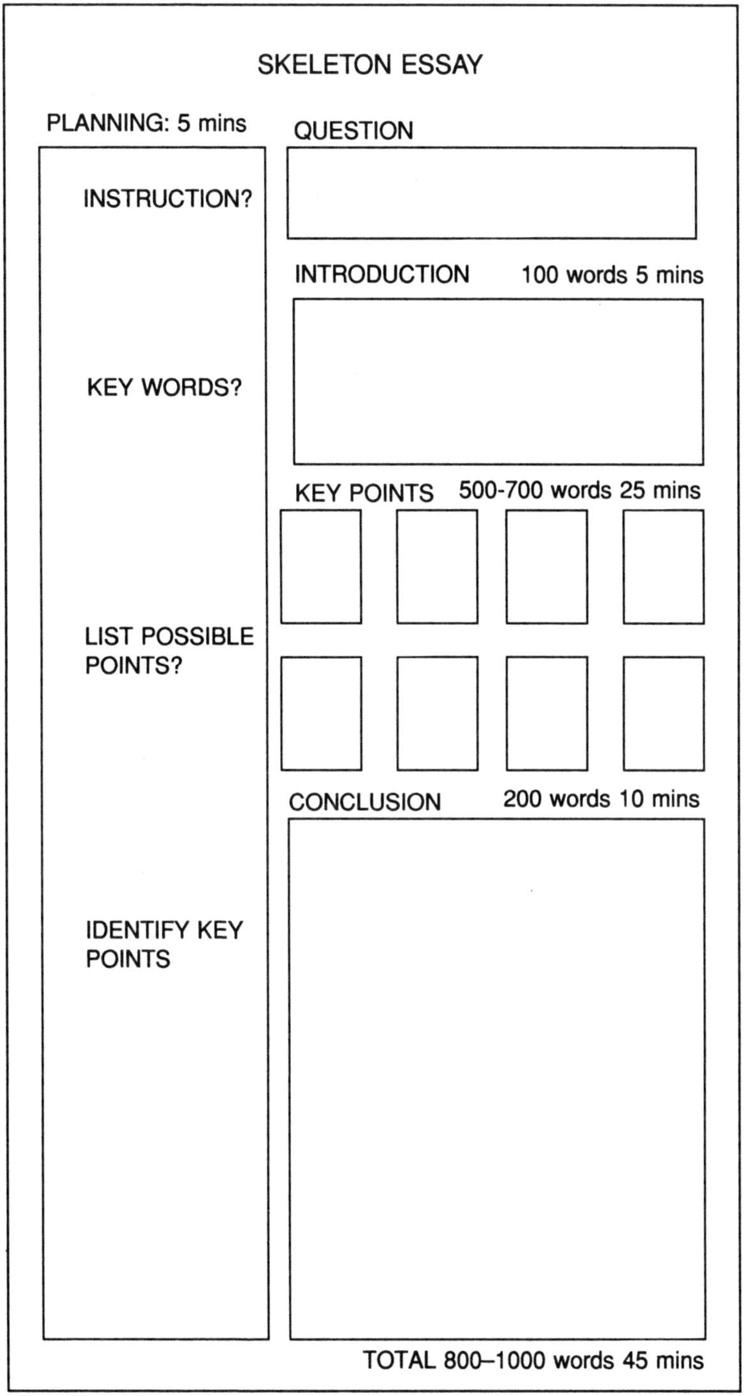

SKELETON ESSAY

PLANNING: 5 mins

INSTRUCTION?

KEY WORDS?

LIST POSSIBLE POINTS?

IDENTIFY KEY POINTS

QUESTION

INTRODUCTION   100 words 5 mins

KEY POINTS   500-700 words 25 mins

CONCLUSION   200 words 10 mins

TOTAL 800–1000 words 45 mins

Fig. 30. Writing skeleton essays.

SITTING YOUR EXAMINATIONS

Exams do mean stress and pressure but if you have completed a full revision programme then you still control the examinations and not the other way around.

Pre-exam checks

Ensure that everything goes smoothly by checking:

- the examination **dates**
- the **start times**
- the **location**
- which **exam paper** and which topics
- **travel times** to ensure early arrival.

Exam checks

Once in the exam room avoid chatter and concentrate on the exam by:

- Setting out pens, pencils *etc* as permitted. (Note that pens with different barrels, *eg* smooth, hexagonal, fat, will ease the pressure on your finger tips. Try using a different pen for each essay.)
- Make sure you can see the clock or set your watch on the desk.
- Check the instructions on the front of the exam paper. How many answers from each section *etc*?
- Scan all of the questions and place a tick against possibilities.
- Do not rush in! Study the question. Plan your answer.
- Write your answer to the 45-minute essay time plan.
- If you run out of time then write a skeleton essay answer.

Good luck does help with examinations but hard work is even better, so hopefully you will get your reward and gain good results.

CHECKLIST

Achieve your full potential in the examinations by:

- investigating the demands of the examination
- studying past examination papers

- studying the examiners' reports
- listing the examination requirements
- identifying the key revision topics
- setting a revision schedule
- collating key topic notes
- condensing key topic notes
- creating key cards
- writing skeleton essays
- checking all examination arrangements.

CASE STUDIES

Susan opens the post

Susan raced to the front door as she heard the post thud onto the hall mat. A brown A4-sized envelope immediately caught her eye and she opened it to reveal five sets of past Chemistry A-Level examination papers. They had only taken a week to arrive from the examining board.

Susan sat at her desk and carefully ruled a revision topic table and entered all of the exam years down the left hand column. Next she put all of the key topic areas across the top of the table. She scanned all of the questions in the first exam paper and wrote the relevant topic area against each one in pencil. It was then an easy task to copy all of the questions into the table.

When the table was complete Susan could see that some topics had an exam question every year and so were a must for revision, whereas other topics had only been examined once or twice in five years. The different questions on the same topic also highlighted how important the key words of each question were. Susan prepared a revision list to discuss with her tutor. It was money well spent.

Mohammed collates advertising

Mohammed pinned the list of nine key revision topics for A-Level Communications onto his bedroom wall and noted that 'Advertising' was the first topic. He pulled all of his notes on advertising out of his file and read through all of them while sipping a cup of coffee. Mohammed set his mug down and finished reading. It was quite a straightforward topic and all of his notes made sense. He flipped open his new revision notes file and inserted all of his advertising notes into one A4 plastic sleeve for safe keeping. Finally, he took his pen and ticked the 'collated' box on his revision list against the topic of advertising.

'Revision underway!' smiled Mohammed.

Yasmin counts the weeks

Yasmin sat at the kitchen table with the wall calendar spread out counting the weeks to 24 May. She had entered her first exam, A-Level General Studies, but the rest followed swiftly afterwards.

'How many?' asked her mother as she dried the dishes.

'I make it 20 weeks once term restarts in January,' replied Yasmin.

'So what do you have to do?' enquired her mother.

'Don't waste any of the weeks,' replied Yasmin. 'January to collate all of my notes, February and March to condense the notes and April and May to write and learn my key cards.'

'What are you talking about?' laughed her mother.

'It's called being organised,' replied Yasmin returning the calendar to the kitchen notice board.

John writes a skeleton essay

Essay writing had always been a mystery to John and something he had never been good at but he found the skeleton essay technique worked for him. It broke an exam essay down into simple steps and he quite enjoyed sitting with his watch timing the writing of introductions. After writing introductions to five different essay titles on the same topic he was really proud of his ability to lift the key words and in only five minutes use them to write a clear, sharp introduction. It gave him considerable confidence to know that he could do it.

DISCUSSION POINTS

1. What concerns do the examiners regularly express in their formal reports?

2. Isn't revision best left to a month before the exams so it is immediate and fresh in your mind?

3. How do you personally revise and learn information best?

12
Acting on Your Results

```
AUGUST

 1   2   3   4   5   6   7
 8   9  10  11  12  13  14
15  16  17 (18) 19  20  21
22  23  24  25  26  27  28
29  30  31
```

A-Level results are published every mid-August on a Thursday. Your school or college will be able to specify the exact date to circle on your calendar. Try and ensure that you are not on holiday as you may need to act on your results.

COPING WITH YOUR RESULTS

Take comfort from the fact that few students receive exactly the grades they had expected. There will be ups and downs but 'downs' will affect your university application and will dictate some immediate actions.

Passing with expected grades

If your grades match your university offer or better then relax, congratulate yourself and get your bags packed! There is no need for you to inform the university as all universities receive the results direct on the Monday of the results week. You will receive a letter confirming your university place from UCAS normally within a week of the publication of the results and must return your acceptance of the place within seven days.

Passing with marginal grades

If your grades are marginally beneath your university offer then there is a danger that you may be rejected. The universities will first sort and confirm all acceptances and will aim to consider all marginal cases by the first Tuesday after publication of the results. Take action to try and secure your place by **writing a letter** to the relevant admissions officer and making a case for acceptance. Ask your tutor to support your case and endorse your letter or to send the letter on your behalf. Most colleges and schools will have a fax machine or use first class post. If there are convincing reasons for your marginal performance then it is highly likely that you will still be offered a place. A letter is best in these circumstances as the telephones will be jammed with calls and when your case is reviewed your letter will be in front of the admissions officer. Keep your fingers crossed and wait for a letter from UCAS which should arrive within a week of the results. Hopefully, you will receive an acceptance, but if not UCAS may have other offers for you through the clearing process. If you receive no offers then proceed as for low grades.

Passing with low grades

Absorb the shock and don't punish yourself too harshly! Look back to the A-Level grade boundaries given in Chapter 10 and note that the loss of only 7/8 marks could turn high expectations into low results. The minimum entry requirement for some degree courses is two Grade Es so there is a course somewhere for you but you will have to find it!

Many universities will have vacancies at the Grade E level and above and will advertise all of their vacancies starting on the first Sunday after the results and thereafter every Wednesday and Sunday. Look for the adverts in the quality newspapers and visit your local careers office as they will have access to the Educational Counselling and Credit Transfer Information Services (ECCTIS). This is the university computer database which lists every university vacancy. It is quick and easy to interrogate and will give you a printout of all vacancies in a given subject. Some colleges and schools have their own ECCTIS link and of course familiar staff to assist you, so do check.

You may have to change your course expectations but be cautious and discuss the courses available with careers staff or your tutors. The expansion of higher education has led to a profusion of new degree courses often linked to narrow vocational areas or at the opposite extreme broad, disconnected courses. Find out about employment prospects and the graduate employment record before dashing headlong into an unusual degree course. Draw up a short-list of possibilities from the adverts, check the prospectuses in the careers library and then leap on the telephone. UCAS will contact you by letter within a week of the results and will enclose your Clearing Entry Form (CEF). You will need to refer to this when you telephone so keep it handy. The switchboards will be jammed with calls so you may need to keep trying all day and possibly for several days before getting through to the relevant admissions officer. Be prepared to sell yourself over the phone and hopefully you will be made an informal offer. The offer will be confirmed once your CEF is received by the admissions officer so do not delay and post first class.

Finally, there is no correlation between A-Level results and final degree results so go forward with confidence and gain a good degree.

Passing only one A-Level

If you pass only one A-Level you might consider joining a Higher National Diploma course (HND). The entry standard is one A-Level pass but think carefully before you apply and particularly ask about student destinations and the level of employment success. HND courses are two-year courses with a vocational theme and they are available in universities and in some colleges of further education.

Only apply if you are committed to seeking employment in the relevant vocational area as the course will emphasise practical work-related skills and knowledge. It is possible in some universities to transfer to a related degree course after one year or after you have completed the course depending on your progress.

FAILING YOUR A-LEVELS

This will be a shock but it is not the end of the world! There are always options. Look back to the grade boundaries listed in Chapter 10:

- Grade N – Narrow Fail
- Grade U – Unclassified Fail

If you obtained Grade N results then only a few marks separated you from passing with a Grade E or even D.

Did a particular exam or question not go well?

It could so easily have been the other way around and so perhaps your best option is to retake your A-Levels.

If you obtained Grade U in one or more subjects then this implies a very low exam performance and you will have to be certain of the reasons for this. Discuss your performance with your tutors and analyse what may have gone wrong. If the results were unexpected then a retake may again be the best option. However, be absolutely certain of your commitment and ability before taking a repeat course and if you have any doubts then it may be best to seek employment.

Retaking A-Levels

You could choose to retake your A-Levels as follows:

- return to school or college

- attend your local college of further education

- enrol on a correspondence course

- join adult education evening classes

- enrol in a specialist tutorial college or 'crammer'.

The **tutorial colleges** have a good record of success as they specialise in one year, intensive retake courses with small classes and individual attention guaranteed. However, the fees can be high and few exist outside the major cities. If you are interested look for adverts in the quality press in August and September. Many schools and colleges also offer good retake programmes so check carefully what is on offer in your local area. Particularly check if the syllabi will remain the same as a change may confuse. Remember that the careers service will give you neutral advice and will have information on all of the options in your area.

APPEALING AGAINST YOUR RESULTS

If you are shocked by the appearance of Grade N or U results then this is an issue to discuss with your tutors as the basis of a possible appeal.

Mistakes by examining boards are thankfully rare but they do happen. You should be concerned if your results are below:

- your GCSE base prediction

- your predicted grades

- your mock exam performance

- your tutor's expectations.

If this is the case it may be a good idea to appeal. Only private candidates may appeal direct to the examining board and all other candidates must apply through their school or college. Ask your tutor for support and complete an appeals application form. There are different levels of exam rechecks available with progressively higher fees as follows:

- Clerical recheck: for a small fee (£2/4) the board will ensure that your grade has been properly recorded.

- Re-mark: a chief examiner will re-mark your examination papers and confirm or alter the grade. Expect to pay around £35 for this service.

- Re-mark and report: as above but with a written report reviewing your exam performance and explaining the marks. This will cost approximately £50.

The services and fees will vary slightly from board to board but your school or college will be able to give you exact information. The **closing date** for appeal applications is 30 September each year so act without delay, but be prepared to wait up to two months for the result.

The majority of appeals do fail and the original grades will more than likely be confirmed, but if you are retaking A-levels the examiner's report will be valuable information in pinpointing your mistakes.

AVOIDING FAILURE

Hopefully you will have read this chapter while you are still in your first year or at the start of your second year of A-Levels. If so absorb this glimpse of your possible future and take steps to ensure that you pass and gain the grades you need by:

- organising a study base

- working with your tutor

- developing your study skills

- reviewing your progress

- implementing the 20-week revision programme.

Follow the guidance given in each of the chapters of this study guide and be a:

STUDY MANAGER!

Good luck with your university course and future employment.

CHECKLIST

Act on your final A-Level grades, as necessary, by:

- defending your grades if marginally lower than expected
- chasing university vacancies if your grades are low
- considering an HND course if you pass only one A-Level
- appealing to the examining board if your grades are significantly below expectations
- seeking advice from your tutors and the careers service
- retaking your A-Levels if appropriate.

CASE STUDIES

Susan is delighted

Susan accepted the envelope from the sixth form secretary and gritted her teeth. Even though she was expecting good results it was still a nerve-racking moment.

'Open it!' urged Catherine, her best friend.

Susan tore the envelope open and her eyes scanned the small computer slip.

'Maths A,' read Susan.

'Biology A and Chemistry A,' she gasped.

'Three Grade As, that's brilliant!' exclaimed Catherine.

'I don't believe it,' replied Susan, shaking her head.

'Believe it,' stated Catherine. 'You worked for it and earned every mark. What did you call it?'

'Acting as a Study Manager,' grinned Susan.

Mohammed protects his place

Mohammed looked again at his results slip but the grades had not changed.

'Well?' asked David, one of his classmates.

'I'm disappointed,' replied Mohammed, 'Grade B in English Language, a B in English Literature, but only a C in History.'

'Disappointed!' exclaimed David. 'Those are very good results.'

'But they may not be good enough for my university who wanted three Bs.'

'Get on the phone?' suggested David.

'No I'll ask my History tutor to write a letter of support and post it today,' replied Mohammed.

'Did you send a letter?' asked David when he spotted Mohammed later in the day.

'Yes, and my History tutor was able to list my mock exam grades and normal range of essay marks for the admissions staff to judge against the lower than expected grade.'

A week later Mohammed saw the postwoman walking up the garden path and waited by the door. He eagerly opened the letter from UCAS and was delighted to receive a confirmed offer of his university place.

Yasmin exceeds her expectations

Yasmin was beaming with joy as she absorbed how well she had done. She never considered herself brilliant or clever, just well organised and hardworking. At best Yasmin had expected Grade Bs but not two As and two Bs.

'Is it good then?' asked her mother, studying Yasmin's face as she climbed back into the car.

'Grade As in Sociology and Psychology and Grade Bs in Government and Politics and General Studies,' boasted Yasmin.

'Congratulations!' exclaimed her mother, 'but you deserve it, you and your 20-week revision programme.'

'Yes, it worked, it really did work!'

'Dinner out tonight, I think?' suggested her mother.

John scrapes home

John knew before he opened the envelope that his grades would not be good. He knew that his Economics exam had not gone well but he had still hoped for better grades.

'Economics, Grade N, Computing D and Law E,' he read again to himself.

He felt depressed and regretted his lack of revision. Looking back he had started off well by planning a revision programme but he had not kept to it. Going out with mates had seemed so important at the time.

'Bad news?'

John looked up to see his personal tutor standing in front of him.

'Yes, I'm really stuck.' said John, 'my university offer was CCD and I've blown it!'

'You've not blown it,' comforted his tutor. 'You've passed two A-

Levels which is a good achievement, so let's make the most of it.'

John sat in his tutor's office and scanned the printout of university vacancies from ECCTIS.

'This course looks interesting,' considered John.

'Add it to the list of possibilities,' instructed his tutor, 'and remember that these are just the first early vacancies.'

'What next?' asked John.

'Read up on your short-list of courses from the prospectuses in the careers library, and be patient for a few days. The main vacancy lists will not appear until Wednesday and Sunday in *The Times*, *Telegraph*, *Independent* and *Guardian* newspapers. Also check ECCTIS as the vacancies will change daily.'

A week later John returned to college to see his tutor.

'Well?' questioned John's tutor.

'I ended up with a choice of two universities who were happy to accept my grades,' grinned John.

'Excellent,' confirmed his tutor, 'but now that you have a place be certain that you want it.'

'What do you mean?' asked John.

'I mean only go to university if you have the motivation to work hard otherwise you will only drop out and waste a place.'

'Don't worry,' stated John, 'I won't make the same mistakes twice and I will work hard at university and gain a good degree.'

'Certain?' questioned his tutor.

'Totally,' concluded John, 'and thank you for your help.'

DISCUSSION POINTS

1. Do you think that all university applications should wait until actual results are known in August?

2. If you gain only one A-Level pass which would be best for you:

    (a) join a suitable HND course?

    (b) retake your A-Levels?

3. How can you ensure that you pass your A-Levels?

On 27 March 1996 Sir Ron Dearing published his long awaited report into post-16 education and, in particular, A-Level.

The Dearing Report runs to 700 pages and makes 200 separate recommendations for improvement. The Secretary of State for Education, Gillian Shephard, accepted the report in full. Some recommendations will be implemented immediately from September 1996 but most will not be implemented until September 1997 at the earliest.

A-Level is firmly endorsed as the key national qualification and it will form the heart of a new National Diploma qualification along with Advanced GNVQ courses which will be renamed Applied A-Levels. The key change for A-Level students will be the opportunity to undertake a much broader programme of study and to develop wider skills of more direct relevance to employment. To understand the need for reform it is important to appreciate some of the existing criticisms of A-Level.

CONSIDERING CRITICISMS

A-Level is our best known and a widely respected national qualification but it is often misunderstood and misapplied. It was originally introduced to prepare students for university and this is a job it performs extremely well as A-Level subjects provide a narrow, in-depth specialism which is carried forward into university. This is the strength of A-Level but it is also its Achilles heel, as the following points make clear:

- A-Level is regarded as 'best' and is attempted by too many unsuitable students who either fail or drop out early. Dearing estimates that some 80,000 students gain nothing from A-Level each year and this is a huge national waste of talent and ability.

- A-Level is attractive because it is viewed as a passport to the 'best' jobs, meaning professional occupations, but the wealth of the nation is derived from industry and business and A-Level devalues practical, employment-based skills and trades. This perpetuates an academic vocational divide in British education and society which is unhealthy.

- A-Level promotes a narrow curriculum and allows students to specialise too early and drop key subjects.

- Humanities students often possess very low numeracy and IT skills.

- Science students often possess very low literacy skills.

- All students possess very low oral presentation skills.

- There are too many syllabus options.

- The standards vary too much between subjects.

- The brightest students are insufficiently stretched.

- There is little opportunity to transfer between courses.

- AS-Levels have not succeeded as two-year courses.

- Science and Maths enrolments are in decline with a drop from 29.8 per cent of students in 1984 to 16.6 per cent of students in 1995.

- Records of Achievement are undervalued.

- Students leaving at the end of the first year have nothing to show for a whole year's work.

These criticisms reflect a need to improve A-Level and to ensure that Britain's future workforce is able to meet the challenge from our industrial competitors particularly Japan and Germany. The government has set national achievement targets for the year 2000 as follows:

- 60 per cent to gain two A-Levels or equivalent.

- 85 per cent to gain five GCSEs at grades A to C.

The current 1996 figures are 44 per cent and 63 per cent respectively. Britain has only a few years left to reach a target that the people of Japan and Germany have already surpassed! Consequently there is a need for reform to produce a more literate, numerate, articulate and technologically aware workforce if Britain is to compete successfully in world markets.

LISTENING TO THE CUSTOMERS

Dearing invited the National Foundation for Educational Research (NFER) to canvass opinion for reform. They collated 850 responses to a questionnaire covering schools, colleges, universities and employers. Many of the above criticisms arose from this research. One point of agreement between A-Level and GNVQ students was that coursework was positively endorsed as opposed to exam-only courses.

- 93 per cent of A-Level students supported coursework.

- 98 per cent of GNVQ students supported coursework.

In addition, research into A-Level examination results over the past three years confirmed what many people have suspected for years, that some A-Levels are easier to pass than others. The following table lists the top ten hardest and easiest A-Level examinations to pass in rank order:

Hardest subjects	*Easiest subjects*
1. Maths	1. Art
2. Chemistry	2. Home Economics
3. General Studies	3. Design and Technology
4. Physics	4. Classical Studies
5. French	5. Communications
6. German	6. English
7. Economics	7. Business Studies
8. History	8. Computer Studies
9. Biology	9. Religious Education
10. Spanish	10. Geography

Dearing has recommended further research into these differences with the aim of ensuring that the same standard of achievement exists for all A-Level subjects within the next five years.

Overall, a mass of evidence was collated and Dearing consulted widely before arriving at some key recommendations.

REORGANISING THE FRAMEWORK

Dearing investigated not just A-Level courses but the whole provision for 14–19-year-old students which encompasses some 16,000 qualifications. To make sense of this wide range of courses, Dearing proposes three clear qualification pathways:

- work-based vocational training
- school/college-based vocational training
- academic courses.

The qualifications available within each pathway will be divided into four achievement levels:

- entry
- foundation
- intermediate
- advanced.

This reorganisation of courses and levels should allow for easier comparisons between different qualifications and it reflects the existing National Vocational Qualification (NVQ) levels. A student on a particular pathway will progress from level to level and enjoy parity of esteem with the other pathways in a move calculated to reduce the academic/vocational divide. The pathways may be different but the standards achieved at each level will be comparable. One key part of Dearing's proposals are for common links to be established between the courses on each level to allow for easy transfers from one course to another. Once in operation this should be a very clear and easy to understand framework for all post-16 education and training.

IMPROVING A-LEVEL

Dearing has endorsed A-Level as the standard to be achieved for the new National Advanced level given above. In recognition of this,

GNVQ courses which currently form the basis of the school/college-based vocational pathway will be renamed Applied A-Levels. This is essential to overcome the belief that GNVQ is second best. GNVQ will in the future operate at A-Level standard but in Applied or vocational subject areas. One will not be better than the other. They will simply represent different qualification choices depending upon career interests.

The specific improvements to A-Level will be as follows:

- All academic A-Levels will have the same standard of achievement.

- All examining boards will ensure the same standard between boards.

- Advanced Supplementary (AS) Levels will be renamed Advanced Subsidiary levels and they will be designed to be taken at the end of the first year of a two-year A-Level course, Academic and Applied.

- The number of resits for modular courses will be restricted.

- All subjects will involve a final examination of at least 30 per cent.

- 'S' papers will be encouraged to stretch the most able.

- Degree modules may be offered to the most able.

- Common curriculum links will be established between Applied and Academic A-Levels to allow for easy transfers in the first year.

- A new AS Level in Key Skills will be introduced.

Basically A-Level will remain the same but with some more quality checks to ensure a consistent standard across all subjects. The major changes which will affect A-Level students will be the introduction of Key Skills and National Certificate and Diploma courses.

Key skills

Concern has been expressed for decades by employers about the low standards of basic numeracy, literacy, oral skills and more recently IT skills of students seeking employment.

A-Level may provide a detailed knowledge of three subjects but all too often employers are not making job offers on the basis of subject knowledge but are looking for an ability to:

- research information
- write reports clearly and concisely
- work with figures
- interpret and draw graphs
- speak fluently and with confidence
- present information
- participate in meetings as a team member
- be self-motivated
- work without supervision
- take the initiative.

These skills are often more important that subject knowledge to employers and here GNVQ has the advantage over A-Level as it focuses upon the development of these skills whereas in A-Level it is more haphazard.

This issue was first addressed in November 1989 by the then Secretary of State for Education, John McGregor, who instructed schools and colleges to seek ways of adding the following core skills to A-Level courses:

- communication
- numeracy
- IT
- personal and social skills
- business and enterprise skills
- foreign languages.

There were some successes in individual colleges but no formal method emerged of how to record or assess core skills other than by a Record of Achievement, and the initiative faded away.

The Dearing Report has renamed core skills as 'Key Skills' and specified only three:

- Communication
- Numeracy
- IT.

However, the wider core skills are addressed by the term 'Community Studies' and this may involve the study of:

- teamwork
- problem-solving
- self-management

- citizenship
- world of work
- parenthood.

The precise method of how best to introduce and assess these wider skills is a matter for consultation but a new AS Level in Key Skills will assist and these skills will be part of the new National Certificate and Diploma courses.

Introducing the National Certificate

A National Certificate will be awarded to students who complete a course of study involving:

- a minimum of two academic A-Levels, *or*
- a minimum of two Applied A-Levels, *and*
- a programme of assessed Key Skills.

This will ensure that all students develop Key Skills and that students, whether following an academic or vocational pathway, qualify with the same certificate and enjoy the same status.

Introducing the National Diploma

The National Diploma repeats the above programme but extends the Certificate into a much broader programme of study by adding AS-Levels to be taken at the end of the first year.

Students would be asked to select four AS-Levels for their first year of study from the following curriculum areas:

- science, technology or maths
- languages
- humanities or arts
- community studies.

The exams would be taken at the end of the first year and would give students who decide to leave some formal achievement. Students in their second year will be able to specialise in two or three of their subject choices and the most able will be offered Special papers (S-Level) or even some degree course modules.

All of the details of the new Certificate and Diploma courses have yet to be discussed and finalised in detail with schools/colleges and examining boards but what is certain is that future A-Level students will face a much broader programme of study.

CONSIDERING A FOUNDATION COURSE

It is possible that some or all of the first year of the Certificate and Diploma courses will become a common Foundation programme with students then choosing Applied or Academic A-Levels for their second year of study. This would make sense and make for a more integrated programme. Some colleges and schools have successfully introduced a common six-week overlap between some A-Levels and GNVQ courses with students receiving detailed careers and subject advice before deciding which course to specialise in. It is this approach which might be extended for a full term or even the whole of the first year.

Dearing has invited the National Council for Vocational Qualifications and the Schools Assessment Council to examine the existing GNVQ and A-Level syllabuses and report upon the possibilities of a common first-year curriculum. 50 per cent of GNVQ students and 43 per cent of A-Level students surveyed were in favour of a common Foundation year.

DEARING REPORT AND YOU!

There will be no significant changes before September 1997, given the need to discuss and develop all of the above new proposals. However, it is certain that the Dearing Report will significantly alter the shape of post-16 education as the proposals have been broadly welcomed and accepted.

You could perhaps introduce your own 'skills audit' and record the skills achieved in your own Record of Achievement. This means considering carefully, and perhaps with your tutor's help, the skills involved in studying your A-Level subjects.

Take a sheet of paper and create three lists of information about each of your A-Level subjects:

1. *Subject knowledge*   List the topics covered by each subject, *ie* what do you know? A general subject label does not convey to employers exactly what you have covered. Take a pride in your subject knowledge.

2. *Subject skills*   List the skills developed in each subject, *ie* research? writing? oral presentations? working in groups? IT? numeracy? Employers

value these skills so record your experience and ability.

3. *Subject careers*   List all of the careers and especially business and industry which might value your subject knowledge and/or skills. Realise that quite often it is your skills that employers want not your subject knowledge, hence the importance of key skills.

Once you have collated all of the above information, demonstrate your IT skills by presenting it all neatly in a Record of Achievement format along with information on:

- social interests
- community involvement
- sports
- work experience.

Even if you have only delivered newspapers, were you punctual and reliable? If so, ask your employer to confirm this in your Record of Achievement.

Look to the world of work and the skills and aptitudes you will need for a successful career and demonstrate that you have the skills and ability. This ultimately is what the Dearing Report is all about, so put it into action yourself and create your own Diploma!

Appendix B

A-LEVEL SUBJECTS

Ancient History
Applied Engineering Graphics
Archaeology
Art and Design
Art History
Bengali
Biology
British Government and Politics
Business Studies
Chemistry
Classical Civilisation
Classical Studies
Communication Studies
Computing
Design and Technology
Economics
English Language
English Literature
Environmental Science
French
Further Mathematics
General Studies
Geography
Geology
German
Greek
Hebrew
History
History of Music
Home Economics
Human Biology
Italian
Latin
Law
Mathematics
Media Studies
Music
Panjabi
Philosophy
Physical Education
Physics
Principles of Accounts
Psychology
Religious Studies
Russian
Sociology
Spanish
Sport Studies
Statistics
Theatre Studies

Stop press!
The AEB is planning to publish syllabuses for A-Level Football, Rugby and Cricket in September 1996.

GCSE A-LEVEL CORRELATION

To predict your A-Level potential first convert your existing GCSE grades to a points total as follows:

GCSE Grade	A*	A	B	C	D	E	F	G	U
Points	8	7	6	5	4	3	2	1	0

Arrive at your GCSE points total by adding your score for:

- English Language
- Mathematics
- Best five other grades or all grades if fewer than five other subjects.

Calculate your potential A-Level points by using the following formula:

(GCSE score x 1.05) minus 29.46.

Alternatively identify your A-Level points total by plotting your GCSE score on the graph given on page 113.

The resulting A-Level points total will give you a broad idea of the A-Level grades you might be expected to reach using standard UCAS points as follows:

A-Level	A	B	C	D	E	N	U
UCAS Points	10	8	6	4	2	0	0

AS-Level points are half of the above points, *ie* 5, 4, 3, 2 and 1. If your GCSE points total is 32 – 35 then you will find A-Level work demanding and below 32 points you should accept careers advice before starting an A-Level course.

Further Reading

All of the following careers reference books will be held by your school or college careers library or by a careers officer or will be stocked by a good bookshop.

INFORMATION AND ADVICE

Occupations '96: this annual volume published by the Careers and Occupational Information Centre provides details on approximately 600 careers. You will find details of pay, qualifications, and range of duties and addresses for further information.

CRAC Publications: the Careers Research and Advisory Centre (CRAC) publishes a whole range of general advice books. Look for: *Decisions at 17/18+* by Michael Smith and Veronica Matthews, *Jobs and Careers After A-Level* by Anne Purdon and *Your Choice of A-Level* by Mary Munro and Alan Jamieson.

Kogan Page Publications: Kogan Page publish individual careers books which cover in detail all aspects of a particular career.

HIGHER EDUCATION GUIDANCE

You can use the following reference books to check the entry requirements demanded for different university degree courses and to obtain general advice and information on the choices open to you.

Complete Degree Offers, Brian Heap – provides a detailed analysis of all of the degree options in the UK.

NatWest Student Book, Klaus Boehm and Jenny Lees-Spalding (eds) (Macmillan Press) – an annual volume providing a student view of the facilities available in each university.

Which University?, Tony Allan (CRAC) – provides a full survey of all university options.

IDENTIFYING EMPLOYERS

Once you have researched a particular career you can locate possible employers from the following reference books:

Key British Enterprises (Dun and Bradstreet) – all of Britain's top 50,000 companies are listed in this six volume reference set with some information about each company.

The Guardian Guide to the UK Top Companies – provides useful information on Britain's major employers.

Dun and Bradstreet – look for a Regional Business Directory to your local area which will provide a full listing of every employer and the nature of their business.

COMPANY RESEARCH

Never go to an interview without first researching the company.

The International Directory of Company Histories (St James Press) – provides a brief history of the development of all major international companies.

The Times 1000 (The Times) – provides a full breakdown of the company organisation and current business statistics.

CD Roms – check current developments by searching *The Times* or *Guardian* newspapers' CD Rom for articles on the relevant company.

GETTING THE JOB

How to Write a CV That Works, Paul McGee (How To Books, 1995).

How to Apply for a Job, Judith Johnstone (How To Books, 1996).

How to Get That Job, Joan Fletcher (How To Books, 1993).

FINALLY!

Do you have your own business idea? Read *How To Start Your Own Business*, Jim Green (How to Books, 1995) and employ yourself.

Useful Addresses

EXAMINATION BOARDS

The Associated Examining Board (AEB), Stag Hill House, Guildford, Surrey GU2 5XJ. Tel: (0117) 927 3434.

East Midlands Regional Examinations Board (EMREB), Robins Wood House, Robins Wood Road, Nottingham NG8 3NR. Tel: (0115) 929 6021.

Northern Examinations and Assessment Board (NEAB), Devas Street, Manchester M15 6EX. Tel: (0161) 953 1180.

Oxford and Cambridge Schools Examinations Board (OCSEB), Purbeck House, Purbeck Road, Cambridge CB2 2PU. Tel: (01865) 54421.

University of Cambridge Local Examinations Syndicate (UCLES), Syndicate Buildings, 1 Hill Road, Cambridge CB1 2EU. Tel: (01223) 553311.

University of London Examinations and Assessment Council (ULEAC), Stewart House, 32 Russell Square, London WC1B 5DN. Tel: (0171) 331 4000.

University of Oxford Delegacy of Local Examinations (UODLE), Ewert House, Ewert Place, Oxford OX2 7BZ. Tel: (01865) 54291.

Welsh Joint Education Committee (WJEC), 245 Western Avenue, Cardiff CF5 2YX. Tel: (01222) 265000.

PUBLISHERS

The following information all relates to the recommended A-Level study aids listed in Chapter 10.

Most of the textbooks listed may be obtained from any major bookshop, *ie*:

- Macmillan Mastering Series

- Penguin Subject Dictionaries
- How To Books
- Letts Study Guides
- Longman Revise and York Guides
- Macmillan Work Out Series.

The other study aids listed may be obtained direct from the publishers as follows:

Philip Allan A-Level Review: Philip Allan Publishers, Market Place, Deddington, Oxfordshire OX15 OSE. Tel: (01869) 338652.

Fast Forward Tapes: Fast Forward, Freepost, 7–9 Palace Gate, London W8 5BR. Tel: (0171) 581 4866.

Richard Ball Publishing, Brassey Street, Birkenhead, Merseyside L41 8BY. Tel: (0151) 653321.

Index

How To Books provide practical help on a large range of topics. They are available through all good bookshops or can be ordered direct from the distributors. Just tick the titles you want and complete the form on the following page.

___ Apply to an Industrial Tribunal (£7.99)
___ Applying for a Job (£7.99)
___ Applying for a United States Visa (£15.99)
___ Be a Freelance Journalist (£8.99)
___ Be a Freelance Secretary (£8.99)
___ Be a Local Councillor (£8.99)
___ Be an Effective School Governor (£9.99)
___ Become a Freelance Sales Agent (£9.99)
___ Become an Au Pair (£8.99)
___ Buy & Run a Shop (£8.99)
___ Buy & Run a Small Hotel (£8.99)
___ Cash from your Computer (£9.99)
___ Career Planning for Women (£8.99)
___ Choosing a Nursing Home (£8.99)
___ Claim State Benefits (£9.99)
___ Communicate at Work (£7.99)
___ Conduct Staff Appraisals (£7.99)
___ Conducting Effective Interviews (£8.99)
___ Copyright & Law for Writers (£8.99)
___ Counsel People at Work (£7.99)
___ Creating a Twist in the Tale (£8.99)
___ Creative Writing (£9.99)
___ Critical Thinking for Students (£8.99)
___ Do Voluntary Work Abroad (£8.99)
___ Do Your Own Advertising (£8.99)
___ Do Your Own PR (£8.99)
___ Doing Business Abroad (£9.99)
___ Emigrate (£9.99)
___ Employ & Manage Staff (£8.99)
___ Find Temporary Work Abroad (£8.99)
___ Finding a Job in Canada (£9.99)
___ Finding a Job in Computers (£8.99)
___ Finding a Job in New Zealand (£9.99)
___ Finding a Job with a Future (£8.99)
___ Finding Work Overseas (£9.99)
___ Freelance DJ-ing (£8.99)
___ Get a Job Abroad (£10.99)
___ Get a Job in America (£9.99)
___ Get a Job in Australia (£9.99)
___ Get a Job in Europe (£9.99)
___ Get a Job in France (£9.99)
___ Get a Job in Germany (£9.99)
___ Get a Job in Hotels and Catering (£8.99)
___ Get a Job in Travel & Tourism (£8.99)
___ Get into Films & TV (£8.99)
___ Get into Radio (£8.99)
___ Get That Job (£6.99)
___ Getting your First Job (£8.99)
___ Going to University (£8.99)
___ Helping your Child to Read (£8.99)
___ Investing in People (£8.99)
___ Invest in Stocks & Shares (£8.99)

___ Keep Business Accounts (£7.99)
___ Know Your Rights at Work (£8.99)
___ Know Your Rights: Teachers (£6.99)
___ Live & Work in America (£9.99)
___ Live & Work in Australia (£12.99)
___ Live & Work in Germany (£9.99)
___ Live & Work in Greece (£9.99)
___ Live & Work in Italy (£8.99)
___ Live & Work in New Zealand (£9.99)
___ Live & Work in Portugal (£9.99)
___ Live & Work in Spain (£7.99)
___ Live & Work in the Gulf (£9.99)
___ Living & Working in Britain (£8.99)
___ Living & Working in China (£9.99)
___ Living & Working in Hong Kong (£10.99)
___ Living & Working in Israel (£10.99)
___ Living & Working in Japan (£8.99)
___ Living & Working in Saudi Arabia (£12.99)
___ Living & Working in the Netherlands (£9.99)
___ Lose Weight & Keep Fit (£6.99)
___ Make a Wedding Speech (£7.99)
___ Making a Complaint (£8.99)
___ Manage a Sales Team (£8.99)
___ Manage an Office (£8.99)
___ Manage Computers at Work (£8.99)
___ Manage People at Work (£8.99)
___ Manage Your Career (£8.99)
___ Managing Budgets & Cash Flows (£9.99)
___ Managing Meetings (£8.99)
___ Managing Your Personal Finances (£8.99)
___ Market Yourself (£8.99)
___ Master Book-Keeping (£8.99)
___ Mastering Business English (£8.99)
___ Master GCSE Accounts (£8.99)
___ Master Languages (£8.99)
___ Master Public Speaking (£8.99)
___ Obtaining Visas & Work Permits (£9.99)
___ Organising Effective Training (£9.99)
___ Pass Exams Without Anxiety (£7.99)
___ Pass That Interview (£6.99)
___ Plan a Wedding (£7.99)
___ Prepare a Business Plan (£8.99)
___ Publish a Book (£9.99)
___ Publish a Newsletter (£9.99)
___ Raise Funds & Sponsorship (£7.99)
___ Rent & Buy Property in France (£9.99)
___ Rent & Buy Property in Italy (£9.99)
___ Retire Abroad (£8.99)
___ Return to Work (£7.99)
___ Run a Local Campaign (£6.99)
___ Run a Voluntary Group (£8.99)
___ Sell Your Business (£9.99)

How To Books

___ Selling into Japan (£14.99)	___ Use the Internet (£9.99)
___ Setting up Home in Florida (£9.99)	___ Winning Consumer Competitions (£8.99)
___ Spend a Year Abroad (£8.99)	___ Winning Presentations (£8.99)
___ Start a Business from Home (£7.99)	___ Work from Home (£8.99)
___ Start a New Career (£6.99)	___ Work in an Office (£7.99)
___ Starting to Manage (£8.99)	___ Work in Retail (£8.99)
___ Starting to Write (£8.99)	___ Work with Dogs (£8.99)
___ Start Word Processing (£8.99)	___ Working Abroad (£14.99)
___ Start Your Own Business (£8.99)	___ Working as a Holiday Rep (£9.99)
___ Study Abroad (£8.99)	___ Working in Japan (£10.99)
___ Study & Learn (£7.99)	___ Working in Photography (£8.99)
___ Study & Live in Britain (£7.99)	___ Working in the Gulf (£10.99)
___ Studying at University (£8.99)	___ Working on Contract Worldwide (£9.99)
___ Studying for a Degree (£8.99)	___ Working on Cruise Ships (£9.99)
___ Successful Grandparenting (£8.99)	___ Write a CV that Works (£7.99)
___ Successful Mail Order Marketing (£9.99)	___ Write a Press Release (£9.99)
___ Successful Single Parenting (£8.99)	___ Write a Report (£8.99)
___ Survive at College (£4.99)	___ Write an Assignment (£8.99)
___ Survive Divorce (£8.99)	___ Write an Essay (£7.99)
___ Surviving Redundancy (£8.99)	___ Write & Sell Computer Software (£9.99)
___ Take Care of Your Heart (£5.99)	___ Write Business Letters (£8.99)
___ Taking in Students (£8.99)	___ Write for Publication (£8.99)
___ Taking on Staff (£8.99)	___ Write for Television (£8.99)
___ Taking Your A-Levels (£8.99)	___ Write Your Dissertation (£8.99)
___ Teach Abroad (£8.99)	___ Writing a Non Fiction Book (£8.99)
___ Teach Adults (£8.99)	___ Writing & Selling a Novel (£8.99)
___ Teaching Someone to Drive (£8.99)	___ Writing & Selling Short Stories (£8.99)
___ Travel Round the World (£8.99)	___ Writing Reviews (£8.99)
___ Use a Library (£6.99)	___ Your Own Business in Europe (£12.99)

To: Plymbridge Distributors Ltd, Plymbridge House, Estover Road, Plymouth PL6 7PZ.
Customer Services Tel: (01752) 202301. Fax: (01752) 202331.

Please send me copies of the titles I have indicated. Please add postage & packing
(UK £1, Europe including Eire, £2, World £3 airmail).

☐ I enclose cheque/PO payable to Plymbridge Distributors Ltd for £ [   ]

☐ Please charge to my ☐ MasterCard, ☐ Visa, ☐ AMEX card.

Account No. [   ]

Card Expiry Date [   ] 19   ☎ **Credit Card orders may be faxed or phoned.**

Customer Name (CAPITALS) ....

Address ....

.... Postcode..............

Telephone........................... Signature ....

Every effort will be made to despatch your copy as soon as possible but to avoid possible
disappointment please allow up to 21 days for despatch time (42 days if overseas). Prices
and availability are subject to change without notice.